Leading Grassroots Sports Club

This book brings together all the essential knowledge needed to run, develop and grow a grassroots sports club, in one comprehensive volume.

Offering a structured approach to club development and administration, this book breaks down the complex task of running a grassroots sports club into manageable components. Introducing essential day-to-day and strategic aspects of running a club, it enables sports clubs to select relevant modules according to their current capacity and ambition. This book covers key topics including strategic planning, financial planning, managing facilities, generating income, community engagement, volunteer recruitment, the importance of being a welcoming club and navigating governance requirements. Every chapter includes practical, step-by-step instructions, actionable strategies and templates that managers and volunteers can apply immediately, to help them organise, finance and grow their club, ensuring that even clubs with limited resources or experience can implement best practices efficiently and achieve growth, transparency and long-term sustainability.

Drawing on the author's experience in consulting with sports organisations across the world, this book is essential reading for anybody involved in grassroots sports and is a useful supplementary text for any course on sport business or management.

Geoff Wilson is a Global Sports Strategist and runs his own consultancy – Geoff Wilson Consultancy – with a focus primarily on sport. Geoff has created numerous academic models for the sports industry and has been to over 100 countries in various sports consultancy projects.

Leading a Grassroots Sports Club

A Practical Guide to Managing and Developing Your Club

Geoff Wilson

Routledge
Taylor & Francis Group
LONDON AND NEW YORK

Designed cover image: Shutterstock/Anton Vierietin

First published 2026
by Routledge
4 Park Square, Milton Park, Abingdon, Oxon OX14 4RN

and by Routledge
605 Third Avenue, New York, NY 10158

Routledge is an imprint of the Taylor & Francis Group, an informa business

© 2026 Geoff Wilson

The right of Geoff Wilson to be identified as author of this work has been asserted in accordance with sections 77 and 78 of the Copyright, Designs and Patents Act 1988.

All rights reserved. No part of this book may be reprinted or reproduced or utilised in any form or by any electronic, mechanical, or other means, now known or hereafter invented, including photocopying and recording, or in any information storage or retrieval system, without permission in writing from the publishers.

For Product Safety Concerns and Information please contact our EU representative GPSR@taylorandfrancis.com. Taylor & Francis Verlag GmbH, Kaufingerstraße 24, 80331 München, Germany.

Trademark notice: Product or corporate names may be trademarks or registered trademarks, and are used only for identification and explanation without intent to infringe.

British Library Cataloguing-in-Publication Data
A catalogue record for this book is available from the British Library

ISBN: 978-1-041-09489-0 (hbk)
ISBN: 978-1-041-09488-3 (pbk)
ISBN: 978-1-003-65036-2 (ebk)

DOI: 10.4324/9781003650362

Typeset in Aptos
by KnowledgeWorks Global Ltd.

Contents

List of Templates and Checklists   vii

Introduction   3

1. **Governance and Admin:** Getting the foundations right when running a club   9
2. **Club Planning:** Developing a roadmap for your club   53
3. **Club Experience:** Offering the best experience at your club   79
4. **Coaching Culture:** Getting the right coaching culture at your club   101
5. **Female Participation:** Increasing female participation at your club   109
6. **Protecting Your Club:** Building a positive reputation for your club   119
7. **Community Engagement:** Becoming more focused on the community   127
8. **Communication and Brand:** Getting your communications and image right   143
9. **Income Generation:** Bringing money into your club   173
10. **Facilities:** Making the most of the club's facilities   199

Appendix: Templates and Checklists   209
Index   251

Templates and Checklists

209 Club development framework model
210 Is this guide for you?
211 Action log List
212 Checklist of policies
213 Safeguarding checklist
214 Accident report form
215 Emergency details form
216 Conflict of interest register
217 Risk register
218 Pre-development plan checklist
219 Club development plan
221 Swot analysis
222 Stakeholder analysis
223 Resource analysis
224 Vision statement
225 Mission statement
226 Values development
227 SMART objectives
228 Game-day experience
229 Code of conduct (coaches)
230 Code of conduct (players)
231 Code of conduct (volunteers and spectators)
232 Training session planner
233 Coaches qualification record
234 Checklist for starting a women's team
235 Community engagement checklist
237 Community engagement plan
238 Brand words
239 Brand checklist
240 Annual content planner
241 Digital inventory checklist
242 Website assessment checklist
243 Event calendar

Templates and Checklists

244 Post-event evaluation
245 Game-day planner
246 Income generation calendar
247 Sponsors target list
248 Grant identification
249 Facility plan
250 Facility usage schedule

Introduction

This handbook has been developed for grassroots sports clubs. The handbook is a practical guide that will help to develop and strengthen your club. Don't be overwhelmed by all of the tasks and activities in this book. Resources and volunteers will both play a crucial role in delivering the various elements of this and all parts of the handbook. If you don't have the volunteers to count on, don't worry: Just select the key elements relative to your club's current situation and implement those first.

Who Is the Handbook for?

The handbook is primarily aimed at grassroots sports clubs. For the purpose of this book, grassroots sports refer to adults, youths and children playing sports where they do not get paid. In essence, they play in competitive and non-competitive leagues and tournaments but are not compensated for their participation. Grassroots sports help to nurture talent and provide a pathway to semi-pro or professional sports organisations.

Why Should Clubs Use It?

Clubs ought to follow the advice given in this book as it demonstrates proven methods of how a successful, well-run club should operate.

Those who are elected or employed within the club play an important role in ensuring the organisation is well run, with best practice processes and plans adopted. No matter the legal status of your organisation, clubs must strive to operate professionally with a high degree of transparency and accountability.

The Club Development Framework Model

In any sport, cultivating and enhancing club is crucial. Whether amateur, semi-professional or professional, ensuring long-term survival demands a strategic focus. I've devised a framework model to aid amateur (grassroots) clubs.

While clubs can aspire to embrace the entire framework, it is crucial to note that clubs do vary in terms of ambition, professionalism, size and resources, and as such some pillars will be more applicable than others.

Clubs must prioritize the key pillars based on their circumstances. Expanding into other pillars is encouraged as the club grows and develops.

> You can find the "Club Development Framework Model" in the appendix.

STRENGTH IN NUMBERS

Clubs that rely on one person to manage the different roles and tasks will find it difficult to operate and grow. Sharing the workload with other like-minded individuals (alongside good planning) will ensure you have a well organised and more professional club.

① ② ③
④ ⑤ ⑥
⑦ ⑧ ⑨

How to Use This Handbook

This handbook has *not* been designed to be read from Chapter 1 to Chapter 10. Rather, it is designed for club administrators to select the sections that are relevant to them at any particular time, introducing the various concepts, ideas and templates in order to strengthen or improve the club in that specific situation. Of course, the handbook can be read systematically, but this would take substantial time, and many of the learnings may not be implemented in the club due to the amount of information to consume.

This book aims to break down the challenging job of setting up a club into much smaller, more manageable pieces. The best way to use the handbook is shown in Figure 0.1.

Figure 0.1 How to use this book

REMEMBER

Don't be overwhelmed by all of the tasks and activities in this book. Resources and volunteers will both play a crucial role in delivering the various elements of this and all parts of the handbook. If you don't have the volunteers to count on, don't worry: Just select the key elements relative to your club's current situation and implement those first.

Is This Guide for You?

	YES	NO
Has a club development plan been created & approved by the board?		
Do you have a modern and recently up-to-date club constitution?		
Do you have active committees (action oriented committees who meet regularly)?		
Have you appointed capable and skilled individuals in key roles; chairperson, secretary, treasurer, safeguarding officer, public relations officer, youth/academy/technical director? (the number of roles depends on the size of your club) Have you clearly defined roles and responsibilities for the staff/volunteers?		
Do you have robust financial procedures in place - from annual budget setting to monthly or quarterly income and expenditure accounts?		
Do you communicate with members and key stakeholders on a regular basis (i.e. face to face meetings with parents, coaches, players, fans, local councils etc.)?		
Do you provide ongoing training of staff or volunteers each year, i.e. coach education workshops, good governance, safeguarding training?		

If you have placed a tick in the NO column in the majority of the areas, then this handbook is for you!

You can find a blank copy of "Is This Guide for You" template in the appendix.

Used with permission from Shutterstock/PeopleImages.

Used with permission from Shutterstock/muse studio.

1 Governance and Admin
Getting the foundations right when running a club

> In this chapter you will learn:
>
> 1. The key foundations that should be considered when managing a club
> 2. The importance of good financial management
> 3. To identify the key policies to introduce in your club
>
> Priority areas to adopt in your club after reading this chapter:
>
> 1. Ensure you have the appropriate legal structure
> 2. Ensure your board meets each month with a clear agenda developed
> 3. Ensure you have strong financial reporting in place
> 4. Review and update your club constitution (ensuring it is 'fit for purpose')

What Is Governance and Why Is It Important to Your Club?

Governance focuses on how your club is managed and carries out the processes required to deliver an effective, community-based experience (be that as a player, coach, parent or volunteer).

Good governance is key to a sports club because it ensures transparency, accountability and fair decision-making. It helps the club run smoothly by setting clear rules and responsibilities, making sure resources are used wisely, and keeping everyone – players, staff, coaches, parents and fans – on the same page. With good governance, issues like conflicts of interest or financial mismanagement are less likely to happen, which builds trust and helps the club grow in a sustainable way. Plus, it creates a positive environment that attracts talent, sponsors and community support.

Why Do Clubs Need to Understand the Concept of Governance?

Put simply, governance provides a foundation for any sports club to:

- Protect the club and provide clear transparency and processes to follow should issues arise
- Sustain itself over the medium to long-term
- Provide a safe and enriching environment for everyone
- Attract new members and retain existing ones
- Attract external support and resources including funding
- Hand over the reins in even better shape than it was handed on to you

Good governance is a series of pillars or foundations that provide the basis for a strong and effective sporting organisation when brought together.

What Pillars or Foundations Do You Need to Put in Place for Good Governance?

1. LEGAL STATUS
What is the legal status of your club?

2. STRUCTURES
Have you put the right structures in place? AGM, board, committees, workforce management

3. CONSTITUTION & POLICIES
Have you an up to date constitution, policies and procedures in place?

4. LEGAL COMPLIANCE
Are you compliant with the laws of the game, laws of the land (i.e. data protection)?

5. CONTROLS
Have you financial and risk management controls in place?

6. CLUB DEVELOPMENT PLAN
Have you a clearly defined roadmap or plan in place?
Refer to Chapter 2

KEY PRINCIPLES:
Underlining the 6 pillars are the key principles of honesty, transparency, openness and accountability.
(All staff and volunteers should operate with the above principles in mind.)

Used with permission from Shutterstock/matimix.

1. Legal Status

When establishing your club, the members will need to select the most appropriate form of legal structure for the organisation to be formally recognised, open a bank account, enter into agreements for hiring facilities, and be accountable to the membership.

There are several formal, legal club structures for sports organisations. The type of structure you choose to adopt for your club will depend on the purposes for which it is formed. The key areas to consider when identifying the most suitable legal status include:

- Owning or leasing property
- Applying for grant funding
- Limiting the liability of the board members.

The most common types of structures are:

1. **Limited company (by guarantee):** This is a separate legal entity which can hold property in its name. It has articles of association and also has to be registered with your local government. A limited company (by guarantee) does not have shareholders, but instead has members who vote on elections to the board and constitutional issues such as amendments to the articles. Members are entitled to attend members' meetings and vote. This includes the right to appoint and remove directors.

2. **Limited company (by shares):** Shareholders own the company and is a separate legal entity. This structure is more suited to organisations that want to generate a profit or pay shareholder's dividends.
3. **Unincorporated association:** An unincorporated association is a common structure for sporting clubs. The members come together and agree to establish the club with its own rules and operating procedures. For legal purposes, the club is regarded as a voluntary coming-together of its members—literally, an association of members. This structure suits small sports clubs that do not hold any significant property or employ staff. It's the most common type of structure for a grassroots club.
4. **Community benefit society:** This structure is for the clubs set up for the benefit of community. Profits are not distributed among members and are instead reinvested into the club or used to support projects within the community.
5. **Charitable incorporated organisation (CIO):** This is where the club is registered as a charity. The club is registered with the country's Charity Commission. Trustees rather than directors will run the club. The members of a CIO are not liable for its debts or other liabilities if the CIO is wound up.

Please note, numerous other legal structures exist. The above are some of the more popular structures.

IMPORTANT - The legal structures will differ from country to country. It is vital to understand your country's various legal structures and select the one that best suits your specific need and future direction.

Used with permission from Shutterstock/PeopleImages.com - Yuri A.

2. Structures

This section covers the following 'club structures':

i. The club membership
ii. The board
iii. Committees
iv. Workforce/volunteer management

i. The Club Membership

All club office bearers should be familiar with their legal obligations under the requirements of the relevant governing body and the club's constitution. While these requirements vary from country to country, at the basic level the club is required to hold at least one AGM per year. The AGM is an important event for every club as it gives its members a broad overview of the organisation's financial health, the opportunity to vote on key areas such as amendments to the constitution and the appointment of members to the board.

The main reasons for holding an AGM are:

- To consider the club's annual report
- To elect officers
- To discuss and vote on amendments to the constitution or club rules
- To present the annual accounts
- To present the chairperson's annual report.

A well-run AGM will report to the club's membership on the previous year's activities, allow for the election of the new board or committee members for the year ahead and other business relating to the successful running of the club following the governing bodies' rules.

A club's constitution will document the voting rights of each member. The most significant concern is understanding who can vote on key matters and forming a quorum at AGMs/SGMs (Special General Meetings). A club board has a responsibility to provide this information to its members. The board will ensure that everyone knows their ability, or non-ability, to vote on certain aspects of the club at any meeting.

Five Steps for Running a Successful AGM
1. **Announcement of AGM:** Generally, AGMs should be announced to members one month in advance, with details of the proposed date, time and venue of the meeting, and no later than a specified annual date e.g. 30th June. Some national governing bodies have this as an absolute requirement within their rules and it's worth consulting your club constitution to ensure that your club's AGM is called in line with club rules. The venue for the AGM will vary depending on the size of the club but there should be adequate space to allow for a broad general

attendance of the membership. It should also be possible to hold the AGM virtually. The club secretary is usually responsible for announcing the AGM and this announcement can be distributed to members in writing, via email or using other available means of communication such as social media, club communications apps and physical posters in the premises of the club.

2. **Preparing reports:** The outgoing board or committee is responsible for organising the AGM and reporting on the year's performance in terms of finances and membership activity. Collating this kind of information into a presentable format can be a time-consuming effort, so give plenty of time in advance of the meeting to prepare and review the reports. A financial report, also known as the treasurer's report, looks at the financial data for the club normally across a three-year window, allowing for quick comparison to determine whether the club is performing better or worse than the previous years.

3. **Sticking to the agenda:** Documenting and distributing the agenda is a key part of the planning process for a meeting – depending on your club constitution, members should receive the agenda and related documents (reports) ten days in advance of the AGM. The onus is on the Chair to ensure the meeting follows the agenda and a steadfast Chairperson is required to ensure the meeting progresses as intended. A board or committee member should also take responsibility for minutes at the AGM, as a record of proceedings for future reference. Most club constitutions also require a quorum (a minimum viable number) of members to be present for the meeting to take place; this might be a percentage of the overall voting membership (e.g. 20%) or similar; otherwise, the meeting must be adjourned and rescheduled.

   A proposed AGM agenda can be:
   - Apologies
   - Previous minutes
   - Chair's remarks
   - Presentation of key achievements during the year past/annual report
   - Chairpersons report
   - Finances
   - Proposed agenda items/motions
   - Appointment of auditors
   - Board appointments (if any up for re-election or appointment)
   - Final summary
   - Close

4. **Set and communicate membership fees:** Membership fees and the categories of club membership, along with any additional costs such as member levies, are set at the AGM. In order to vote at an AGM, a member would usually have paid their fees in full for the year in question.

5. **Electing of the board:** The AGM is the time to revitalize the club's board by electing new club officers (chairperson, PRO, secretary etc.); this can bring a new energy to the running of the club as a fresh set of ideas and approaches are introduced. Your club will already have criteria for nominating members to serve on the club's board.

Ensure that these criteria are known in advance (e.g. nominees may have to be nominated by two fully-paid club members). It's important that these procedures are followed correctly in advance of any vote at the AGM. It's important to recognise the role of the outgoing board; volunteering is too often an undervalued (yet vital) role in sports clubs and whoever takes on the mantle as an outgoing or incoming club officer should be appreciated for their efforts. Independent scrutineers should be appointed when voting is being done to offer another layer of transparency.

Annual Report

A club's annual report provides members with an operating snapshot for the previous 12 months. It provides an opportunity to appreciate the efforts of all volunteers and members and to proudly formalise their achievements each season.

Conveying sporting achievements allows members of the club and the wider community (sponsors, politicians, governing bodies, etc.) to be involved in aspects of the club that they generally would not encounter.

It also helps unite and reaffirm the vision and mission of the club.

The key areas that an annual report should include are:

- Chair notes
- Outline activity and key achievements in the past year
- Financial figures
- Fundraising activities and sponsors
- Appointments within the club
- Plans for the year ahead

Used with permission from Shutterstock/David Maynard.

ii. The Board

The Role of the Board

Your club's constitution and rules should set out the club structure concerning the board and/or committee of management. A club's board enables the organisation to be run effectively by applying good governance principles and practices. It is recommended for sports clubs to have smaller skill-based boards with greater use of committees.

The board in a grassroots sports club plays a vital role in overseeing the club's overall direction and making key decisions. The board is responsible for managing finances, setting the long-term plan, ensuring the club complies with rules and regulations, and maintaining a strong governance throughout the organisation.

Board Composition

The board should comprise people with an appropriate range of skills, such as:

- Having the ability to think strategically
- Be financially literate
- Commercial, Media and Marketing skills
- Legal & Governance experience
- Coaching experience
- People/Human Resources knowledge
- Project & Facility Management skills

Ultimately they should:

- Be a team player
- Be ethical, honest and trustworthy
- Care about the club and community

TIP

Ensure your club has a diverse board with relevant skills, knowledge and experience.

THE ROLE OF THE BOARD IS TO:

- Set objectives, define policy and develop strategic direction
- Incorporate good governance and ethical standards into daily activities
- Specify the responsibilities of the chair, executive officer (whether paid or volunteer) and board
- Ensure the executive officer (if you have one) provides satisfactory leadership, planning, organisation, control and succession
- Monitor the performance of management and volunteer teams
- Monitor the performance of the organisation against the agreed goals and objectives
- Manage communication with members and other key stakeholders including the State sporting organisation, government, sponsors, etc.
- Ensure all risks are identified and managed appropriately
- Ensure compliance with policies, laws and regulations
- Approve, monitor and review the financial performance of the organisation

TIP

Conduct an audit of the parents, players and coaches in your club. Identify their current jobs and key skills. Put this key information in an excel sheet. Can you utilise them for certain tasks in the club?

Board: Key Areas to Consider

- **Appointment and selection of board members:** For grassroots clubs, a limit of two terms of three or four years per term is preferred to ensure that the board maintains a level of consistency in decision-making, stability and be held accountable for policy and strategy. A staggered rotation system for board members is advisable so that all the knowledge will not leave the club at once.
- **Board diversity:** Evidence suggests that diversity on boards leads to better board performance. A diverse board considers demographic characteristics including gender, age and cultural background, as well as specialist knowledge, skills, ability and social and educational background.
- **Board size:** There are no hard and fast rules regarding board size. It should be appropriate for the size of the club. Five to ten is a good rule of thumb for a grassroots club.
- **Ethics and code of conduct:** Your club should consider developing a code of conduct that defines acceptable standards of personal behaviour, including the conduct of the board.
- **Role and function of the Chair:** The Chair manages meetings, ensures that the board is balanced, maintains open discussion, and includes all directors in the

discussions. It is also the Chair's responsibility to ensure that relevant issues are included in the agenda and that all the board members receive timely information ahead of meetings.

- **Performance appraisals of board members:** The Chairperson should conduct regular board member evaluations to assess their effectiveness.
- **Succession planning and recruitment:** Recruiting board members or volunteers across the club with the appropriate skills and expertise is important and often very challenging for many organisations. The club should consider future board members among its current players, supporters, parents and coaching teams. They should do this by conducting an audit of the skills within the club. In addition, clubs should consider future club Chair's in terms of succession planning.
- **Engaging young people:** Your club should engage with future club leaders by involving young people in your club's management and day-to-day operations. Young people can bring new energy, creativity, enthusiasm and a fresh perspective to the management of your club. They are also typically more flexible and willing to adjust to change. If your club is wondering who will carry it into the future, the reality is that it will probably be your younger members.
- **Committees:** Committees should relieve the board of certain tasks, capitalising on the specialist skills of people in the club willing to contribute their time and expertise. Committees should create 'terms of reference' and circulate minutes of each meeting to the board. Examples of committees include Income Generation Committee, Academy Committee and Finance Committee.

Used with permission from Shutterstock/zieusin.

TIPS FOR RECRUITING NEW BOARD MEMBERS

- Brainstorm the list of skills that are required on your board i.e. marketing, financial etc. Use the table below to identify skills gaps in your board:

Areas of skill/expertise required on the board	Does our club have these skills?	Rate priority 1 – urgent 2 – not important	Action Required by Chair
Commercial	No	1 – urgent	Recruit a person with commercial or sales expertise for the board
Financial & Accounting	Yes	NA	
HR & staffing	Yes	NA	

- The Chair should analyse the skills of the players, coaches, volunteers, fans and parents. The analysis should also be extended to individuals in the community where the club is located. This analysis will also include a greater understanding of the personality of each person to ensure they are the right fit for your club based on your organisations values.

- The Chair should approach key individuals to see if they are willing to volunteer as a board member. It is important to clearly identify the role and the time required. Clubs should try to limit the amount of time required each month for volunteers to avoid burnout. The club should consider setting a time limit for volunteers of 7-10 hours per month.

- New board members should be given an induction to help them settle into their new position. This may include an overview of the role of the board, overview of the club structure, review of key documents such as finance reports, strategic plan, various policies (conflict of interest, code of conduct etc) the constitution, dates for the board meetings during the year etc.

REMEMBER

The Chair should conduct an annual 1:1 with all board members regarding their performance and identify areas where training is required.

Planning for a Board Meeting

Before the Meeting

- Read the minutes from the previous meeting as soon as received and ensure all actions are carried out (make sure all actions are contained within an action log list – check out the appendix for the "Action Log List" template.
- Agree the agenda items at least a week to ten days prior to the meeting. A typical agenda could be:
  - Welcome
  - Apologies
  - Conflicts of interest
  - Approval of the previous minutes. Additions or amendments to the minutes of the previous meeting (which have been circulated with the agenda)
  - Agenda items (for example, finance reports, sub-committee updates, strategic plan updates, major projects i.e. facilities project, any other business)
  - Date of the next meeting (usually at the end of the meeting)
- Set a realistic time allocation for each agenda item.
- Distribute agenda to all people attending the meeting (with brief details and actions against each item).
- Distribute any additional information to be read prior to the meeting.
- Read all the background information before attending the meeting.
- Let the secretary know in good time if you are unable to attend the meeting.

During the Meeting

- Make sure the meeting starts on time – even if people are running late.
- Stick to the agenda.
- Let people express their opinions, but keep things on track and stick to the agenda.
- Listen to the opinions of others and encourage participation from all members.
- Once a decision is made on a topic, move straight onto the next topic.
- Identify actions from the meeting and record them on the action log list.
- Summarise final decisions.
- Draft an agenda for the next meeting and agree on a date, time and location.
- Make sure the meeting finishes on time.

After the Meeting

- Prepare minutes (including actions from the meeting) for distribution ASAP. Minutes should be sent within seven to ten days of the meeting.
- Start to move on the various actions ahead of the next board meeting.

Board Minutes

Best practice for minute taking involves a 'minutes secretary' taking notes, or using a technological solution, i.e. a digital recorder, which then converts to a Word document.

A minutes secretary does not replace the club secretary. The minutes secretary can be anyone who will accurately record the minutes and provide a first draft with speed and efficiency for the board. If you don't have the resources for a minute secretary, then taking the notes from the meeting will fall to the club secretary or an appointed board member.

The club secretary should check the minutes for accuracy and release them to other members for approval.

The minutes should simply provide a useful and transparent record of the meeting's proceedings; minutes do not need to include all points of discussion but rather summarise and provide the resultant decision.

Motions, decisions and other formal aspects are to be noted. The following points are very important.

> For all motions and actions, a named person is assigned and date to be completed is recorded in the minutes.

> Minutes must be disseminated electronically to the committee within seven to ten working days of the meeting.

> If a delegate or committee member presents anything to the board, the document, actions and outcomes must be provided within the minutes.

> The secretary, on behalf of the board, maintains a record of key decisions and an action log list, as below. The action log should be reviewed at every board meeting.

An example of action log is shown in Figure 1.1.

ACTION LOG LIST EXAMPLE

Action Number	Action	Person Responsible	Completion date	Status (not started, in progress, completed)
1	Organise a training session with the coaches in the academy in Dec (this will be a knowledge-sharing workshop)	Sam Wilson	31 Dec	in progress

Figure 1.1 Action log list example

> You can find a blank copy of the "Action Log List" template in the appendix.

Board Roles and Responsibilities
The following outlines the key roles of a board at a grassroots sports club:

Role of the Chairperson
The chairperson typically has the most senior, official role in the sports club and fulfils a range of duties dealing with the overall management of club affairs. The chairperson leads meetings and plans the overall development of the club in the medium to long term.

What Are the Duties of a Club Chairperson?
The chairperson and the board are responsible for the overall, long-term direction of the club and represent the organisation at key events or meetings. The Chair would also manage the board meetings, ensuring that the various agenda items are covered and fully debated each month.

What Are the Typical Traits of a Club Chairperson?
The chairperson role is usually filled by those experienced in positions of leadership. The chairperson needs to be a good communicator, a strategic thinker, and someone able to delegate duties successfully to different volunteers while motivating those volunteers to serve the best interests of the club. Being a good Chair requires not taking over the meeting, but facilitating discussion. This means creating an atmosphere where board members can debate, struggle with issues, reach compromise and sometimes agree to disagree.

The Role at a Glance
The following is an overview of the tasks fulfilled by a club chairperson:

- ❖ Chairing meetings, including regular board meetings and the club AGM
- ❖ Upholding the club constitution, policies and national governing body regulations
- ❖ Delegating, leading and motivating club volunteers towards club goals/objectives
- ❖ Representing the club at key external events or meetings
- ❖ Organising training for the board members throughout the year
- ❖ Organising annual performance appraisals with each board member

TIPS FOR BEING A GOOD CHAIR

☑ The key to successfully chairing a meeting is to be absolutely clear about the purpose of the meeting.

☑ Ensure that everyone knows the rules of the meeting. Is it a formal or an informal meeting? Will decisions be made through consensus or will a formal voting procedure be followed?

☑ Ensure that everyone has an opportunity to speak.

☑ If someone dominates or diverts the agenda and is derailing a meeting, it is up to the Chair to bring them to order.

☑ The chair should acknowledge all members by name.

☑ A good Chair practices active listening. The Chair should allow adequate time for a full discussion but at the same time keep an eye on the time. No one likes long meetings.

☑ When a topic has been fully discussed, the Chair should summarise the main points and put the item to the meeting for a decision or a vote. The Chair should make sure the outcome of the vote is recorded.

Role of the Club Secretary

The primary role of the club secretary in a grassroots club is to provide administrative support to the chairperson and board. Much of the hands-on administrative effort may be delegated to other club officers and volunteers, but the secretary is responsible for ensuring the overall, well-run club administration.

What Are the Duties of the Club Secretary?

The role of the club secretary is pivotal and one of the most time-consuming roles in a club; the secretary must work in tandem with the chairperson, the club treasurer, board members and volunteers/staff each month. The club secretary is also responsible for coordinating club meetings such as the AGM. Finally, the secretary is normally the key contact between the club and the governing body.

What Are the Typical Traits of a Club Secretary?

Club secretaries undertake and coordinate various tasks and, as such, should be very well organised. A high standard of verbal and written communication is also important as it is required for running effective meetings. The role of club secretary requires dedication and a detailed knowledge of applying and adhering to the rules of the club/club constitution and those of the governing body.

The role of secretary is a high-profile role, with a major influence on the overall efficiency and organisation of the club, as well as coordinating different volunteering roles. This requires a considerable degree of flexibility (e.g. taking phone calls during their working day) and as a result this may suit people who operate their own businesses or people who work part-time.

Common Tasks of a Club Secretary

Organising Meetings

- Plan club meetings with the chairperson and agree the agenda.
- Circulate details of meetings (time, location, agenda etc.) to club members.
- Take minutes and circulate to meeting attendees (in the case of there being no separate minutes secretary).
- Follow-up with relevant parties on key actions arising from meetings.
- Ensure meetings adhere to procedures of the club constitution (e.g. quorums and election procedures).

Club Correspondence and Communication

- Initiating and responding to all club correspondence (dealing with queries, official governing body correspondence etc.).
- Filing all club correspondence (incoming and outgoing).
- Adhering to governing body rules on communication (e.g. format/timing of response to written communications).
- Compiling reports for the AGM.

General Administration

- Managing club membership, registration and team affiliation.
- Keeping an accurate record of contact details for members, officers and third parties.
- Handling club insurance and related paperwork (e.g. filing of injury claims).
- Maintain appropriate records of membership and communication, along with club documents such as the club constitution.
- Assist the chairperson in strategic planning of ongoing club development.

Role of the Club Treasurer

The treasurer is responsible for overseeing the flow of money into the club and for allocating and recording how that money is spent. This is a vital role as the treasurer works to ensure the club can meet its day-to-day expenses and prompts the need for increased club fundraising when a shortfall in income exists. The treasurer also works in conjunction with the chairperson in planning the development of the club, e.g. creating annual budgets, estimating funds required for a capital project, like a new playing surface or clubhouse, and projecting membership and income for future years to contribute towards prudent planning of the club's future.

What Are the Typical Traits of a Club Treasurer?

Like any position responsible for handling money, the treasurer is expected to be transparent and honest in their dealings on club business. Good record-keeping is essential and, while a background in finance or accounting is not imperative for this role, it is preferable to have someone who is experienced in managing accounts. This role is often filled by small business owners, accountants and other professionals who manage money (e.g. bank officials).

The Role at a Glance

The club treasurer typically manages the club's finances, reports on the club's financial performance and spearheads the fundraising effort (alongside the fundraising committee) to ensure that the club has the necessary funds to continue operating. The treasurer takes responsibility for the following:

- ❖ Creating and maintaining the club's annual budget.
- ❖ Working with other club officers to generate and collect membership funds.
- ❖ Ensuring accurate and up-to-date records of all club income and expenditure.
- ❖ Making payments to third parties.
- ❖ Preparing and issuing invoices.
- ❖ Managing the club's bank account.
- ❖ Paying staff/coaches salaries and expenses.
- ❖ Seeking approval of the club's board for major expenditures.
- ❖ Preparing financial statements ahead of the AGM.
- ❖ Reporting on the club's financial performance at the AGM.

Role of Club Directors

The club directors should be aware of their individual roles on the board. These will include:

- ☑ Financial management (this involves understanding the financial position of the club)
- ☑ Volunteer management
- ☑ Risk management
- ☑ Member protection and equality
- ☑ Workplace health and safety
- ☑ Judicial process and dispute resolution
- ☑ Disciplinary issues
- ☑ Legal matters including working with children, police checks, child protection and safeguarding and data protection
- ☑ The upkeep of codes of behaviour, conduct, equality and antibullying
- ☑ Facility management
- ☑ Strategic management

iii. Committees

The Role of Committees

The main role of committees is to dive deep into a specific area and provide the board with additional insight.

It is vital to make sure that these meetings are kept short, to the point and are completely necessary for the operation of the club. Otherwise, you may lose the interest of the members.

Suggested Committees

Committees should relieve the board of certain tasks.

A typical sports club may require the following committees:

- **Income generation committee:** To explore and secure revenue streams and funding for the club
- **Promotions/Media committee:** To market and promote the club in the community
- **Sporting/Technical/Coaching committee:** To oversee technical areas such as coach development, competitions, etc.
- **Academy/Youth committee:** To oversee all areas related to underage involvement, including academy program, non-competitive blitzes, camps, age structures in the academy etc.
- **Facility committee:** To oversee and ensure the facility is fit for playing and hosting sport

The Chair of any sub-committee should be a member of the board.

TIPS

Don't have too many committees in your club.

Each committee should have a written 'terms of reference'.

Used with permission from Shutterstock/Magagina.

REMEMBER

It's important you have the right people on your committees who have a clear understanding of the committees' purpose.

Composition of Committees

The committees should comprise people with an appropriate range of skills.

Important areas to consider:

- Clear description of the role, tasks and responsibilities of each committee
- Clear description of required competencies of members
- Clear understanding of the relationship between the board and committee

The above should be outlined in a 'terms of reference' (ToR) document. A ToR document will include:

- Purpose of the committee
- Objectives of the committee
- Membership of the committee and Chair of the committee
- How members will be appointed and for how long
- Frequency of meetings
- Quorum required
- Decision-making authority (if any)
- Reporting to the full board

> **TIP**
>
> Establish a facility, venue or stadium committee which will be responsible for the upkeep and cleanliness of the facility.

iv. Workforce/Volunteer Management

Job Descriptions

Sports clubs should endeavour to generate detailed job descriptions for each role held at the club. Even if your club is an amateur organisation, having a job description for each role is still important. This could be a simple one-page document.

A job description should outline the following:

- A clear list of tasks and directions for their role
- A list of essential skills required to complete the job
- A clear statement of who the position reports to and any decision-making authority

These job descriptions can be adjusted per the needs of the club, and as circumstances change and are aligned with the organisation's strategic plan.

Care should be taken to adhere to employment laws in your country when hiring staff, and in the case of any recruitment issues.

Volunteers

Clubs can provide a great opportunity for people to develop their own skills while volunteering time and resources for your club. People are the lifeblood of clubs and your most valuable asset. Club committees should proactively manage their volunteer workforce. Coaches, officials and other volunteers need ongoing support, such as induction, training and recognition.

Successful clubs are run by enthusiastic and knowledgeable people who contribute and feel valued.

Spread the Workload

It is vital that you don't let one or two volunteers do all the work. The work should be shared within the club. A good rule is to ensure volunteers only dedicate a small number of hours per week to their role. Volunteers should not go over this set limit. If more time is required to do the role, then more volunteers must be sought. Limiting the amount of time spent at the club will help to prevent burn out and help to retain great volunteers.

One member of the club's committee should have 'volunteer management' as part of their portfolio.

Volunteer Coordinator

A volunteer coordinator is the first point of contact for all volunteers, encouraging individuals to help at the club and organising support and training for those who offer their time. In a grassroots sports club, this role is often covered by board members, who support one another to ensure the club's effective running. Recognition, support and acknowledgement of the contributions of volunteers are imperative in ensuring people feel valued and appreciated.

The responsibilities of the volunteer coordinator are to be:

- Pro-active with the recruitment and training of volunteers
- Show volunteers around the club and make them feel welcome
- Explain what volunteers are required to do and offer feedback/training
- Manage the workload of volunteers and match their skills/experience
- Listen to and address any concerns that volunteers have
- Recognise and reward the achievements of volunteers

Used with permission from Shutterstock/Master1305.

Training for Club Volunteers

A volunteer coordinator should ensure that all new volunteers are given a basic induction to the club, an introduction to the board and other volunteers, and an understanding of what is expected of them. New volunteers should ideally be given a written description of the expected task (this could be by email or as a one-page job description). The volunteer is likely to be a parent and, in order to make them feel comfortable, they could be invited to shadow another volunteer/parent initially for their first session, so they understand the role better. If a reasonable number of volunteers start at the same time, e.g. at the start of the season, the club could consider undertaking a group induction for all, ideally with a social element attached, to thank the new volunteers and make them feel part of the club.

Thanking Your Volunteers

Saying thank you to volunteers goes a long way towards keeping everyone happy, motivated and willing to continue devoting their efforts. Volunteers don't do it for pats on the back but, without them, there would be fewer clubs running today, so appreciation is a must. Some top tips for thanking the volunteers at your club are:

- ❖ **Say thanks to volunteers in person:** It may appear obvious but regularly congratulating each other and fostering an environment where even the unglamorous tasks that are ticked off get a glowing mention will go down well.
- ❖ **Thank volunteers collectively:** Being praised in a group communication (like a club-wide email or on the clubhouse noticeboard) is another way to flag the work of someone who has excelled themselves.

❖ **Have an annual or monthly volunteer awards:** Some clubs have an annual barbeque or event, where volunteers are nominated and celebrated. Doing something less formal but more regularly (monthly or quarterly) is another route to take. It could be a meal out, cinema tickets, a shopping voucher or something club related like discounted membership or a free ticket to a black-tie dinner.
❖ **Nominate your volunteers for external awards:** Putting forward volunteers gives kudos and has the advantage of some welcome publicity for both the volunteers and the club.
❖ **Offer a training bonus:** Paying for volunteers to acquire skills through training relevant to the sports club is a way of giving back.
❖ **Personalised thanks:** Thanking volunteers doesn't have to be a grand gesture but personalisation (a considerate birthday card and/or gift) will be appreciated.

Used with permission from Shutterstock/Yuri Hoyda.

Key Skills of a Volunteer Coordinator

❖ Excellent knowledge of the club and its people
❖ Confident, enthusiastic and able to motivate others
❖ Very good listener
❖ Able to build relationships
❖ A doer—someone who gets things done
❖ Team player

> **REMEMBER**
>
> Don't assume people have the skills. Customer service training should be offered to staff and volunteers so they can provide a welcoming culture and positive experience.

TIPS FOR SCREENING VOLUNTEERS

☑ Interview all volunteers (i.e. potential coaches, administrators, committee members). Don't rush to appoint volunteers just because you need them. Take time to select the right ones. It will benefit you in the long term.

☑ Develop a list of questions to ask in interviews. Questions to include are: Why do they want to volunteer, what experience have they in the role they are volunteering for? What are their values (do they align with the club values), what do they know about the club and what skills will they bring to the role?

☑ Ask for a minimum of two references before appointing the volunteer.

☑ Conduct a 'police check' on each new volunteer (in order to identify offences).

☑ Pair up new volunteers with existing volunteers. Provide a mentor or buddy program for new volunteers.

THINK!

Make sure you give new volunteers a good induction to the club (this includes an introduction to the board, history and club values, an introduction to key personnel and the club structure, an overview of the club policies) and ensure they fully understand what is expected of them in their new role at your club.

Tips for Recruiting New Volunteers

☑ Brainstorm the list of jobs that need to be done in the club.

☑ Ask your players if they are willing to volunteer during the annual registration (state their work experience and key skills).

☑ Ask the parents of your youth players if they are willing to volunteer at the start of each season (state their work experience and key skills).

☑ Look outside the club (ask members, players, coaches and administrators if they know anyone who can help within their local community).

THINK!
Having wrong volunteers is worse than having no volunteers at all. It is vital your club recruits the right type of person.

REMEMBER
Conduct training once per year for your volunteers. Training could include first aid, safeguarding, administration duties and coaching.

Roles of Other Key Members in the Club (Outside of the Board)
Some of the key roles that a club should have outside of the board are as follows:

PRO/Communications Officer
The Public Relations Officer (PRO) role at any grassroots club is vital in sharing club information with the general public. The PRO will regularly work with other club officers, coaches and club volunteers to act as the voice of the club when dealing with the media or wider public. The PRO is responsible for giving the public the club's best image; this helps attract new members to the club and keep existing members aware of the latest initiatives, ensuring that members remain engaged in club activities. Refer to Chapter 8 for useful information ideas for your PRO.

Welfare Officer
The welfare officer responds to any concerns over child or adult welfare and ensures robust procedures are in place to protect all children and vulnerable adults. Specific training courses and certification should be offered to the welfare officer. These courses could be held by the governing body.

Fixture Secretary/Registrar
The fixture secretary/registrar is a vital cog in a club's organisation, ensuring that a full programme of fixtures – across all age groups – is in place and fulfilled, including coordinating association competitions and entering teams into the relevant competitions. Your fixtures secretary will attend relevant fixture meetings and communicate these within the club. Many grassroots clubs do not have a dedicated fixtures sectary. This club secretary often performs this role. It is recommended that clubs have a separate person solely focused on fixture management for the club.

THINK!
Don't overload individuals with too much work. Spread the workload.

Academy/Youth Director

It is widely accepted that player retention is vital to any sport and club. One of the main reasons players leave sport is a poor standard of coaching.

As such, clubs are encouraged to appoint their own academy or youth director to enhance the coaching and playing experiences within the club.

What Is the Academy/Youth Director Role?

The primary role of the academy/youth director is to provide relevant and valued coaching support in the club environment and to monitor and mentor coaches to conduct appropriate quality activities that will enhance the players' and coaches' experience.

It is important to recognise that this role is designed to be flexible to meet the particular needs of your club. Therefore, specific areas can be the focus, such as:

- Coaching support
- Recruitment and retention of coaches
- Disseminating information to parents
- Developing a clear club playing style across all age groups

Attributes of an Academy/Youth Director

The following attributes are important when appointing an academy/youth director:

- Minimum 12–24 months' coaching experience
- Well-known and respected individual
- Strong understanding of the national sports curriculum
- Possesses sound organisational skills
- Displays well-developed interpersonal skills, including empathy and caring qualities
- Shows an ability to think on their feet and be proactive

What Does an Academy/Youth Director Do?

☑ Fostering and supporting a positive club coaching culture.

☑ Developing a coach's knowledge and skills.

☑ Monitoring and mentoring club coaches while providing support based on their requirements

☑ Building the confidence of the coach who they are working with.

☑ Being a resource – either sharing their own knowledge or directing coaches to other sources of information.

Governance and Admin

- ☑ Assessing the coach for a qualification, while ensuring that the coaches have access to appropriate resources and development opportunities.
- ☑ Establishing a coach development plan.
- ☑ Presenting parents with relevant information at regular intervals.
- ☑ Liaising with the governing body representatives and attending workshops in relation to the role.

3. Constitution and Policies

This section covers the following:

i. Constitution

A constitution is a set of written rules and objectives, agreed upon by your organisation's members, governing how your club is run.

It will provide direction and guidance to your members and other stakeholders. It formalises the name, objectives, structure/method of management and other conditions in which your club operates. Importantly, it should set out the process for how a person becomes a member of the club, the voting power of each member and the powers of the committee and board in running the club.

Grassroots clubs across the country vary in size, complexity and operation. Therefore, there is some flexibility in how each club may be governed and what is contained in each club's constitution and by-laws.

Used with permission from Shutterstock/Real Sports Photos.

A robust governance framework in a club's constitution provides for accountability, contestability and transparency.

It must also be noted that a club's governing body, at a state, branch, zone or association level, may require certain provisions in its constitution. Their guidance will also be valuable as your club establishes or modifies its constitution. Your club's objectives should not be inconsistent with those of your state or governing body.

WHAT SHOULD BE IN A CONSTITUTION?

1 The name of the club

2 Aims and objectives of the club

3 Membership types (for example some clubs may have full member, associate member, junior member, life membership)

4 Membership fees and dates for payment of fees

5 Officers of the club including how they will be elected and how long in post (i.e. Chair, vice chair, secretary, treasurer, fixtures secretary, PR officer)

6 Names of the various committees, make up of each committee, how often they will meet, decision making powers and how they will report into the main board

7 Club finances & reporting (including who can sign off on invoices/receipts, details around the bank account, the financial year of the club, auditing of accounts, budget process and regular financial reporting to the board)

8 AGM (including notice to members for AGMs, reports to be submitted at the AGMs, nomination to committees/board, voting rights, quorum at AGMs and the right to call EGMs)

9 Details of key policies to be complied by all members, for example, equality, code of conduct, safeguarding etc

10 Discipline and appeals (including areas such as the appeals process, who will sit on an appeals panel, how poor discipline will be dealt with and any right to appeal)

11 Dissolution. This will include the process to dissolve the club and what happens to assets of the club

12 Amendments to the constitution. This outlines the process to amend the clubs constitution and how many votes are required by members

Governance and Admin 37

It is recommended that the club reviews its constitution on an annual basis to ensure it is fit for purpose.

ii. Policies and Procedures

As your sports club grows and develops its range of activities, you will probably find it necessary to establish several club policies and procedures that set out in more detail how the club and its members should operate.

Policies and procedures are used in an organisation to guide decision-making and provide transparency. Irrespective of size, all sporting clubs should adopt a series of basic policies and procedures. Most of these can be re-drafted or directly taken from parent-body documents at state and/or national level.

These policy documents do not have to be complicated or lengthy but they must be communicated to all volunteers, members, parents, coaches, spectators, players and understood by everyone involved. Do you have a notice board? If so, these policies could be printed out and displayed on the notice board and club website.

Policies and procedures are implemented to protect the club, the board and its key stakeholders.

Once policies are in place, they must be regularly reviewed and updated. It is recommended that all policies and procedures are reviewed every 12 months.

THINK

Policies are only as good as the people who use them; the most common mistake made by organisations is not actively referring to their policies to guide decisions.

Checklist of Policies*

Policy	
Child protection	☑
Safeguarding policy	☑
Data protection policy	☑
Equality & diversity policy	☐
Conflict of interest	☑
Recruitment policy	☐
Disciplinary policy	☐
Code of conduct for parents, spectators, volunteers, committee/club officials coaches & players	☐

Anti-bullying policy	☑
Dispute resolution	☐
Date checklist reviewed:	31 July 20xx
Name of person:	Sam Wilson (Board member)

*Feel free to add other policies to the list above.

> You can find a blank copy of the "Checklist of Policies" template in the appendix.

The checklist of policies outlines several important documents to create. The following pages provide further information on several key policies to adopt in your club, including code of conduct, safeguarding, conflict and dispute resolution and managing conflicts of interest.

Code of Conduct

The code of conduct aims to promote and strengthen the reputation of the sport in your country by establishing a standard of performance, behaviour and professionalism for its participants and stakeholders.

In addition, it seeks to deter conduct that could impair public confidence in the honest and professional conduct of games, or in its participants' integrity and good character.

Refer to the appendix for a code of conduct for coaches, players, volunteers and spectators.

Creating a Safe Environment and Safeguarding Members

Those staff members or volunteers who work with children or vulnerable adults must complete a check with their local police. The outcome of a check is either a clearance to work with children/vulnerable adults or a bar against working with them. If cleared, the check will be valid for several years (please confirm with your local sports authority). However, staff and volunteers should be continuously monitored.

Your local sports authority will be able to provide information, resources, tools and online training to increase the capacity and capability of administrators, coaches, officials, players, parents and spectators to assist them in preventing and dealing with discrimination, harassment, child safety, vulnerable adults, inclusion and integrity issues in sport.

Ten Tips for Creating a Child-Safe Organisation

1. Child safety is embedded in sports club leadership, governance and culture.
2. Quarterly parent meetings are arranged with the team's coach.
3. Equity is promoted, and diversity is respected throughout the club.

4. People working with children must be suitably qualified.
5. Processes to respond to complaints of abuse are in place.
6. Staff and volunteers are continually trained and educated.
7. Child-safe standards are continually improved and reviewed.
8. Policies and procedures document how your club is child-safe.
9. Safeguarding training is conducted every year by the club for all volunteers/staff members.
10. Training is provided to coaches on how to coach and communicate with a child.

Safeguarding Checklist

The following is a useful checklist to use when reviewing safeguarding in your club:

	Y	N
Safeguarding policy		
Does your club have a safeguarding policy for the protection of children/young people/vulnerable adults?	☐	☒
Designated safeguarding officer		
Do you have a designated safeguarding officer responsible for all issues regarding the protection of children, young people or vulnerable adults?	☐	☒
Codes of conduct/behaviour		
Do you have written standards of good practice i.e. a code of conduct/behaviour?	☐	☒
Do you have a process to ensure that the code of conduct/behaviour is communicated to relevant parties – volunteers/staff/parents/young people so they are aware of the standards set by your club?	☐	☒
Training		
Do you ensure that your volunteers have access to appropriate safeguarding training? [Note: It is good practice to keep a record of those volunteers/staff who have attended safeguarding training.]	☐	☒
Reporting		
Do you have procedures for dealing with complaints and concerns regarding poor practice, abuse or neglect i.e. clear reporting procedures?	☐	☒
Recruitment		
Do you have recruitment procedures for those working/volunteering with young people that include:		
❖ Completing an information/application form that enables the applicant to self-declare any previous offences; and	☐	☒

❖ Completing a police check (or equivalent) for those working with or responsible for children or young people (i.e. regulated positions)?	☐	☒

Date checklist reviewed: 31 July 20xx

Name of person: Sam Wilson (Safeguarding officer)

> You can find a blank copy of the "Safeguarding Checklist" template in the appendix.

Dealing with an Accident at the Club

Unfortunately, accidents can occur in the club's premises or during games.

The board should have a clearly defined procedure for dealing with accidents at the club. For example:

1. Ensure immediate safety:
   - Stop all activities and ensure the area is safe to prevent further injury.
   - If necessary, evacuate the area and call emergency services if the injury is serious.
2. Administer first aid:
   - Provide first aid using the club's first-aid kit.
   - Ensure a trained first aider handles the situation.
   - Stay with the injured person until help arrives or they recover.
3. Contact emergency services if needed:
   - For severe injuries, call emergency services immediately.
   - Provide clear details about injury, location, and condition of the injured person.
4. Notify next of kin or emergency contact:
   - Inform the injured person's emergency contact if the injury is serious.
5. Complete an accident form:
   - Record details of the incident.
   - Ensure the form is signed and stored securely.
6. Review and prevent future incidents:
   - Investigate the cause of the accident.
   - Implement safety measures to prevent recurrence.
   - Share safety reminders or updates with club members.

> You can find a blank copy of the "Accident Report Form" and the "Emergency Details Form" in the appendix.

> **THINK!**
>
> Appoint several first-aid volunteers within the club and organise training on a regular basis.

> **THINK!**
>
> Make available a first-aid kit for all the teams in the club.

Conflict and Dispute Resolution

Disputes can arise within a club from time to time, and board members are responsible for dispute resolution. It is important for clubs to have clear rules regarding what behaviour is acceptable and a definite process to follow when a dispute does arise. These rules may be contained in the club's constitution, in by-laws or any other formal document that members agree to be bound by, such as a code of conduct.

The dispute resolution mechanisms in place within each club depend on the individual club's needs and capability. However, a club must follow its rules when dealing with any dispute.

Clubs should publish a clear process for their members to raise complaints about other members of the club.

An example of a conflict/dispute resolution process would be:

Step 1: Informal Discussion

- ❖ The parties involved should first try to resolve the dispute through direct and respectful communication.
- ❖ A senior club or board member can help facilitate the discussion if needed.
- ❖ If resolved, no further action is required.

Step 2: Mediation by Club Board Members

- ❖ If the issue remains unresolved, the matter should be brought to the attention of a club board.
- ❖ A neutral party (e.g. club secretary or board member) will mediate a discussion to find a fair resolution.
- ❖ Any agreements should be documented for reference.

Step 3: Formal Complaint to the Club Board

- ❖ If mediation fails, the aggrieved party can submit a written complaint to the club board.
- ❖ The board will review the complaint, gather statements from involved parties, and assess any relevant club policies or codes of conduct.
- ❖ The board will make a decision and communicate it to all parties involved.

Step 4: Appeal Process

- If a party disagrees with the decision, they may appeal to a higher authority within the club, such as a disciplinary or appeals committee.
- The appeal must be submitted in writing within a set timeframe, and a final review will be conducted.

Step 5: Governing Body Involvement

- If the dispute cannot be resolved at the club level, the matter may be escalated to the sport's governing body (e.g., regional/national governing body).
- The governing body may conduct its own investigation and issue a final ruling based on its regulations and disciplinary procedures.

Conflicts of Interest

Conflicts of interest for board and committee members will invariably arise because we all have lives outside of the club. The key is not to allow the role to advantage an individual board member, their relatives or friends. Management of conflict of interest is the key.

Management of conflict of interest is designed to minimize embarrassment or criticism of the board or the individual.

It is often the case that a board member may have a pre-existing conflict and only realise this when the matter is raised in a meeting or after a meeting. This does not matter so long as when a member of the board recognises that a potential conflict exists, he or she advises the Chair immediately if in a board meeting. The following process should be adopted:

Process 1

At the start of every board meeting, the Chair gives all members the opportunity to declare any conflict or raise any concerns regarding perceptions of conflict that may arise in the course of the agenda for that meeting.

Process 2

On being advised of a potential conflict, the Chair acting on the advice of the board, then decides whether:

a. A conflict does not exist.
b. A conflict does exist and agree if the member can remain in the meeting as the board would benefit from the member's experience.
c. A conflict does exist and the member needs to step outside the meeting during the discussion.

Whatever action is taken to manage the conflict, the action needs to be recorded in the minutes.

For ongoing matters where a board member has a conflict, the Chair needs to make appropriate arrangements with the member and others to ensure no impact arises from the conflict. This is recorded in the minutes each time. If the discussion of a conflict of interest involves the Chair, then a temporary Chair needs to be appointed by the rest of the board to manage the discussion (see Figure 1.2).

CONFLICT OF INTEREST REGISTER EXAMPLE

Name of person in the club	Position in the club	Person and / or Organisation with Interest	Nature of Conflict of Interest	Date of Declaration
Lewis Wilson	Chair (Board)	Henry Hamilton of Hamilton Sports (providers of kit, balls)	Hamilton Sport tenders each year to be our kit provider. The owner of Hamilton Sports is a relation of the chair	14 Nov 202x

Figure 1.2 Conflict of interest register

> You can find a blank copy of the "Conflict of Interest Register" template in the appendix.

4. Legal Compliance

Complying with the rules and regulations set by your sport's governing body or league is fundamental for a grassroots sports club's smooth operation and creditability. These rules often cover essential aspects such as the competition rules, fair play and club administration (ensuring that the club operates within the agreed framework of the sport).

Adhering to these guidelines helps maintain the sport's integrity and protects the club from potential sanctions or penalties that could arise from non-compliance.

Beyond the sport's specific regulations, grassroots sports clubs must also comply with broader national laws and regulations, such as General Data Protection Regulations (GDPR) and safeguarding requirements. GDPR compliance, for instance, ensures that the club handles personal data responsibly, protecting members' privacy and reducing the risk of data breaches. This is particularly important in a grassroots setting where trust and community reputation are paramount.

Similarly, adhering to safeguarding regulations is critical for protecting vulnerable individuals, particularly children and young people, who participate in the club's activities. These regulations help create a safe and welcoming environment, ensuring everyone can enjoy the sport without fear of abuse or harm.

Compliance with both sports governance rules and national regulations also enhances the club's reputation and trust within the community.

THINK!
Make sure you are aware of the competition rules each year (in case of any annual amendments to the rules and regulations).

Used with permission from Shutterstock/Anton Vierietin.

5. Controls

This section covers the following:

i. Finance
Clubs should keep accurate and up-to-date records of financial transactions. The exact requirements may vary depending on the legal structure of your club.

Members of the board are directly responsible for ensuring that the finance records are accurate and up-to-date.

Financial Management
Good financial management is essential for your club's survival and is an important part of good governance. Often clubs appoint a financial 'lead' with some accounting experience to take on this responsibility. However, every board member should understand a club's accounts and financial reports.

Governance and Admin

The term 'financial management' refers to the planning, directing, monitoring, organising and controlling of the monetary resources of a grassroots sports club in such a manner to best contribute to helping the organisation accomplish its objectives.

It is good governance to set up a 'finance committee' to help manage the clubs accounts and reporting. The role of this committee should be:

1. Develop the annual budget ready for approval by the board (one more before the start of the next financial year).
2. Develop monthly or quarterly income and expenditure and cash flow reporting for the board.
3. Pay suppliers or any other invoices during the year.
4. Liaise with the bank regarding areas such as online banking and securing loans.
5. Ensure the proper process is followed regarding procurement.

Financial Disclosure

Clubs must keep records that correctly document and explain their financial transactions and financial position.

Your club must adhere to your country's legal requirements for financial reporting.

Financial Reporting and Auditing

Clubs must prepare a financial report to be presented to their members at the AGM.

For clubs, financial management and reporting involves elected and appointed members to the board, treasurers and officers being able to do the following:

- Read and interpret financial statements and consider financial reports and legal requirements
- Examine the types of reports which should be provided to the board
- Reflect on the financial and non-financial metrics which provide knowledge about your club's organisational performance
- Assess the board's responsibilities regarding reporting against legislative and funding requirements
- Effectively manage club funds
- Implement sound financial practices and understand your organisation's financial position and obligations

Setting up a Bank Account
To open a bank account for the club, the following will normally be required:

- ❖ The club's constitution or rules
- ❖ The club's full name and any unique registration documents, e.g. a certificate of incorporation or not-for-profit registration certificate
- ❖ Meeting minutes authorising the opening of a new bank account with details of the individuals authorised to open the account
- ❖ Details of at least two board members (full name, residential address and date of birth)

Generally, two office holders, including the chairperson, or treasurer, will need to visit the branch to open the account. Those setting up the account should decide who will be a signatory on the account, and what account limits to set whereby more than one signature is required in order to spend funds/make a payment or transfer. It is recommended that all transactions require two signatures from board members.

Annual Budget
All clubs, regardless of size, require a budget. The budget sets the financial foundation and direction for the club for the upcoming 12 months/season and aligns it with its longer-term strategic goals. Some clubs may set their budget at zero (where revenues are forecast to completely offset expected expenses in running the club) but other clubs may want to set a profit for the year, especially if the club wishes to have retained earnings for a capital project such as the construction of a new facility.

The annual budget should be approved by the board one month before the start of the next financial year. Check out Chapter 2 for additional information regarding budget setting, including useful templates and processes to follow.

Audited Accounts
It is considered a best practice that a sports club has its financials audited annually. This may or may not be legally required, depending on the status of incorporation.

It is also a best practice that this report is provided with a club's annual report to all members.

Monthly or Quarterly Financial Reports
Creating a quarterly financial report involves summarizing the performance of your club over a three-month period; alternatively, this practice can be performed monthly if required. The quarterly reporting schedule lets you update your club's performance records regularly. This provides your board, suppliers and other stakeholders (e.g. the association or local authority) with the latest financial data to evaluate your club's business track record. Your report should consist of the income statement, balance sheet and cash-flow statement.

Balance Sheet

The balance sheet is one of the three fundamental financial statements (income statement, balance sheet and cash flow statement). A balance sheet reports your business's assets, liabilities and shareholders' equity at a given time.

Balance Sheet Top Tips

- Separate assets (e.g. cash, equipment, sponsorships receivable) and liabilities (e.g. unpaid facility fees, outstanding loans) to ensure clarity.
- Whether cash-based or accrual accounting, maintain consistency to ensure financial statements are easy to understand and compare over time.
- If your club receives grants or donations for specific purposes (e.g. youth development programmes), ensure these funds are recorded separately from general club finances.
- Cross-check bank records with your balance sheet to catch discrepancies early and maintain accurate financial records.

Dealing with Cash

Managing cash is an essential part of good club management. Although managing the day-to-day finances of your sports club can seem a daunting or tedious task, it's a vital part of running a reputable and sustainable sports club. Below are some simple finance practices which will help you manage your club's money and follow good governance standards:

Get Organised and Stay Organised

- Set up a routine that works for you to maintain control of your money month-to-month.
- Check your club bank accounts at the end of every month to monitor what has been paid in and out. If there are any differences, make sure you understand their reason.
- If you have stock (e.g. club kit), make sure you keep detailed stock records and do regular stock takes

Separate Personal Finances

- Keep any personal finances separate from club funds. Don't mix up your personal money with the club's money; at best this is confusing and at worst, it could lead to fraud.
- Keep receipts for all expenses and make sure these are in line with your club's policy on expenses.

Tax

Sports clubs are most likely subject to tax. The tax and amount to be paid will differ from country to country. Tax is usually applied to:

- Purchase of equipment
- Rates on your facility

- Sales of food and beverages from your club bar/shop
- Full-time and part-time staff salaries
- Sales of land or development of new facilities at the club

You may be open to tax relief if your club is a charity or foundation. Contact your accountant or local government to see what tax relief you can avail as a sports club.

Insurance

Grassroots sports clubs would typically look at getting insurance across some of the following areas:

- The club's properties and assets
- Business interruption i.e. loss of revenue/profits
- Legal expenses
- Property
- Group personal accident
- Personal accident
- Directors and officers, covering trustees and committee members
- Public, product and employers' liability
- Special events and tournaments

It is important to understand what types of insurance protection are provided to the club and its members through group policies with regional and national sports bodies. This will help better understand what gaps might exist and where the club needs to purchase additional coverage.

THINK!

Your insurance should cover members, volunteers, officials, parents, spectators, players and visiting opponents

Procurement (Purchase of Kits and Trophies)

It is a best practice to get quotations for items that need to be procured in large quantities, most commonly clothing/kit or trophies/medals for a club.

Your governing body will likely be able to advise on the most reputable suppliers in your region, or your clubs may have some local links. To avoid any negative concern around favouritism, it is recommended to get three quotations, regardless of whether there is a local supplier or not.

It is best to set up a small sub-committee of possibly three persons from the board to evaluate the quotations. The sub-committees recommendations should then be presented to the full board for feedback and input. Through this process, a decision can be made with the board's full support before implementing the decision and advising all participating parties.

Procurement Top Tips
- ❖ Establish a clear procurement policy: Define guidelines for purchasing equipment, services and supplies, ensuring accountability and fairness in decision-making.
- ❖ Obtain multiple quotes for value for money: Compare prices and quality from different suppliers to ensure the club gets the best deal without compromising quality.
- ❖ Maintain transparent record-keeping: Document all purchases, invoices, and approvals to track spending and avoid financial discrepancies.
- ❖ Prioritize ethical and sustainable sourcing: Choose suppliers that align with the club's values, such as local businesses, eco-friendly products, or organizations that support grassroots sports.

Used with permission from Shutterstock/SibRapid.

ii. Risk Management
Risk management involves identifying potential hazards and risks that might occur at any time and implementing measures to mitigate against them.

By identifying and prioritising risks, clubs can prevent or minimise the overall impact of the risk or hazard.

This protects the club and helps build trust with the local community, sponsors and governing bodies. When a club demonstrates a strong commitment to managing risks, it fosters a culture of responsibility and professionalism, ensuring the club's growth and success in the long term.

Process

1. Sit down as a team to identify all the risks (consider all aspects from playing the sport to administration and governance).
2. Prioritise the key risks i.e. top ten.
3. Identify if the risk is likely to happen and what the impact of the risk would be.
4. Identify solutions to mitigate or reduce the likelihood of happening.
5. Insert the risks into the template shown in Figure 1.3.
6. Ensure your board reviews the risks on a regular basis.

RISK REGISTER EXAMPLE

Risk Number	Description of the risk	Likelihood of risk happening (1-5)*	Impact of the risk (1-5)*	Controls / Mitigation	Owner
1	Fire in the clubhouse	3	5	- Update fire alarm etc. - Ensure Fire extinguishers are in the club	George Lee

*1 is highly unlikely, 2 is unlikely 3 is moderate/possible, 4 is likely and 5 is highly likely

Figure 1.3 Risk register

> You can find a blank copy of the "Risk Register" template in the appendix.

Risks to consider when creating your register include:

1. Safeguarding issues
2. Lack of commercial income to the club
3. Loss of players or coaches to other clubs
4. Injury during training or a game
5. Negative PR story on the media
6. Theft of equipment

Governance Checklist*

Clubs should use the checklist below as a useful guide when reviewing their governance and administration in the club:

Do you have the following in place?	Y	N
Annual budget	☐	☐
Monthly or quarterly finance reports (income and expenditure v budget)	☐	☐
Independent audited accounts (annually)	☐	☐
Risk register	☐	☐
Financial & procurement procedures document	☐	☐
Code of conducts – players, volunteers, parents & coaches	☐	☐
Terms limits for board and committee members	☐	☐
Up to date constitution	☐	☐
Organisational chart	☐	☐
Club plan/strategy	☐	☐
Anti-corruption and conflict of interest policies	☐	☐
Safeguarding policies	☐	☐
Process and procedure to appoint the president and office bearers	☐	☐

*Feel free to add other areas to the above checklist.

Final Thought

In this chapter, we outlined the key pillars of good governance for your club, which include establishing legal status, governance structures, a strong constitution, policies, legal compliance, internal controls, and a club development plan. We also discussed the role of the board in driving these efforts and provided an overview of financial management practices. The next steps involve meeting as a club to review this chapter and identify any areas of weakness to address and implement improvements accordingly.

Now you have good governance in place, the next step is to create a club plan that will help you to develop and grow over the following years.

THINK!

Good governance is crucial to get right for a sports club.

Get it wrong and you will be in trouble!

Used with permission from Shutterstock/Drazen Zigic.

2 Club Planning
Developing a roadmap for your club

Having a strong and stable club is important, as it ensures that the club grows and flourishes for years to come. Several matters must be put in place to ensure you have a strong and stable club.

These include, but are not limited to:

- Strong governance
- Great volunteers; from administrators to coaches
- Access to good facilities (i.e. club house, pitches, courts)
- Financial reports and governance policies to help manage the club
- Strong youth structures
- Quality coaching delivered throughout the club
- A clear club development plan

What Is a Club Development Plan?

A development plan is essentially a roadmap for your club. It identifies your vision for the future, goals and objectives, and how the club hopes to achieve them. In short, it is a working document that should be easy to read and provide clear direction for your club.

A club development plan can range from two to five years.

Why Do It?

A development plan is designed to help you prepare for the future. It helps you to have a long-term vision and encourages a coordinated approach to achieve it.

There are a number of reasons why a club development plan is important:

- It provides a clear direction for your club.
- It identifies the key goals/priorities.
- It helps focus your activities during the year.
- It can encourage the involvement of volunteers.
- It ensures the efficient use of resources.

Ultimately, it ensures your club has a future.

Pre-development Plan Checklist

Use the checklist shown in Figure 2.1 before you start the process of creating your development plan.

	YES	NO
Are you affiliated with your governing body?	Yes	
Are your board members up for re-election soon? (It is not good practice to start the development plan process when the chair and board members are up for re-election or are about to step down from the board)	Yes	
Have you elected a club development plan committee and project leader? (A committee that will oversee the development and implementation of the plan)	Yes	
Have you a committee structure in place? Consider committees covering areas such as youth development, income generation, communication etc. This is important as it will be these committees who will help you implement the plan	Yes	
Do you produce an annual budget?		No
Do you produce monthly or quarterly income and expenditure accounts?		No
Do you have a robust income generation plan in place to raise money for the club?	Yes	
Do you have sufficient volunteers and coaches to help you run the club?	Yes	

Figure 2.1 Pre-development plan checklist

If you have answered NO to the majority of the above, it is recommended that you consider actioning these areas before embarking on creating your club development plan.

This will give you a solid foundation from which to create your plan.

> You can find a blank copy of the "Pre-development Plan Checklist" in the appendix.

Planning Your Club's Development

Sports clubs can be developed in many areas. Some to consider in your plan might be:

- ❖ Volunteering
- ❖ Governance and administration
- ❖ Financial management

Club Planning 55

- Youth development/technical plan
- Communication (both digital and traditional/internal and external to the club)
- Income generation
- Development of facilities (either upgrading an existing facility or the creation of a new facility)
- Coach development
- Community engagement

Selecting and prioritising the key requirements is very much down to the club, its current situation and its aspirations for the future.

Creating Your Plan

There are six steps involved in creating a club development plan, as shown in Figure 2.2.

STEP 1: WHO SHOULD BE INVOLVED?

Set up a project team involving the key personnel at the club. A project leader should be assigned to lead on the development of the plan and to ensure the process outlined below is followed.

STEP 2: WHERE YOUR CLUB IS AT NOW

Conduct research of various stakeholder groups, i.e. your spectators, members, players, parents and coaches. This will include 1:1's, focus groups, online surveys and performing a situational analysis. A situational analysis consists of a SWOT, stakeholder analysis, competitor, PEST and resources analysis.

STEP 3: WHERE DO YOU WANT YOUR CLUB TO BE?

Create a vision, mission, values and key goals (priorities) that detail where you want to be in the coming years. Create your SMART objectives under each goal.
NOTE: Use the club development plan template in the Appendix to create your internal document.

STEP 4: HOW DO YOU GET THERE?

Create your SMART (Specific, Measurable, Achievable, Responsibility and Time-Bound) action plans under each objective. Create a budget and organisational chart aligned to your new plan.

STEP 5: WRITING AND DISTRIBUTING THE PLAN

Develop an external facing document that clearly sets out your direction of travel, goals and objectives. This external document will contain high-quality photographs and will take the key information from the internal plan and present it in a professional structure. The external plan should be sent to your local politicians, club members, sponsors and other local agencies.

STEP 6: MEASURING AND MONITORING YOUR SUCCESS

Introduce regular monitoring of the plan regarding the progress against the targets set. This will ensure you continue to move in the right direction and help you to realise when you have achieved something

Figure 2.2 Steps involved in creating a plan

Club Development Plan Example

Figure 2.3 shows a template that can be used by your club. Further details on how to complete each section of the plan will be outlined in this chapter.

OUTLINE THE RESULTS OF YOUR RESEARCH (SITUATIONAL ANALYSIS, FOCUS GROUPS AND SURVEYS)

Notes
- Outline the output from your situational analysis: SWOT, stakeholder analysis, competitor analysis, PEST and resources analysis.
- Outline the findings from your focus groups and 1:1's
- Outline the findings from your survey
- Gain an understanding of your governing body's strategic plans and priorities
- Conduct a review of your current club structure and committees
- Conduct an analysis of the club's financial information
- Conduct an analysis of your player registration/membership data
- Conduct an analysis of all programs you are currently running throughout the year
- Outline the key findings from government and sports reports from your region

OUTLINE THE VISION, MISSION AND VALUE STATEMENTS OF THE CLUB

Notes
- Outline the club's vision (where you are heading, what your ambition is, your North Star!)
- Outline the club's mission (why you exist, what is your purpose)
- Outline the club's values (how you behave as a club)

OUTLINE THE KEY GOALS

Notes
- Outline the broad areas where you will focus your resources and efforts over the term of your plan, i.e. income generation, participation, governance, facility management etc (these will be identified from your research and vision):
1.
2.
3.

OUTLINE THE KEY OBJECTIVES UNDER EACH GOAL

STRATEGIC GOAL EXAMPLE: DRIVE INCOME GENERATION

Notes: Outline your SMART objectives under each goal. For example see below (for each goal there will be one table which outlines the key objectives)

Objective	Key Actions (list the key tasks under each ob)	Completion Date (acheived by)	Responsibility (who is the owner)	KPI/Measure (Target)	W.R.A.G. (is it on schedule)
Secure sponsorship for all the youth teams	• Develop sponsorship package • Develop list of businesses to target • Develop sales presentatior	31 July 202X	Income Generation Officer	$10,000 achieved	🟢
Generate food and beverage revenue on game days	• Identify potential food and beverage suppliers • Agree cost to purchase food and beverages • Agree event calendar to sell food and beverages • Agree team to serve food and beverages. Provide necessary training.	30 September 202X	Income Generation Officer	$10,000 achieved	🟢

OUTLINE HOW THE PLAN WILL BE MONITORED THROUGHOUT THE YEAR

Notes
- Outline how the strategic plan will be monitored, i.e. quarterly reports presented to the board

PEOPLE & FINANCES

Notes
- Outline the organisational chart / various committees that will deliver the plan. Outline the income and expenditure covering the period of the plan.

Figure 2.3 Club development plan

You can find a blank copy of the "Club Development Plan" template in the appendix.

Step 1: Who Should Be Involved?

Getting the Right People

The development of the plan depends on a small group of people with specific skills and knowledge. A club development committee should be set up comprising of, for example:

- Project manager (leader of the club development plan process)
- Chair of the club
- Selected board members
- Technical or youth/junior director/manager
- Parents/players who have experience in business management, strategic planning
- Selected coaches from the club

Although the club development committee will lead the process, members, players, parents, coaches and sponsors must be all involved, where possible. This can be achieved during step 2 of the process – the research stage.

Used with permission from Shutterstock/Juice Flair.

REMEMBER

Organise focus groups with the following stakeholders to gain a deeper understanding of where you club is at: spectators, players, coaches, administrators in the club.

Step 2: Where Your Club Is at Now

Doing Your Analysis

Once you have set up your club development committee, the next stage is to identify where the club currently stands. The best way to achieve this is to:

- Conduct a **SWOT analysis**.
- Conduct a **stakeholder analysis**.
- Conduct a **resource analysis**.

> You can find a blank copy of the "SWOT Analysis", "Stakeholder Analysis", and "Resource Analysis" templates in the appendix.

- Conduct research with your members, parents, coaches and players – through **focus groups, 1:1's and online surveys**.
- Conduct a review of your current club structure and committees. In addition, analyse the effectiveness of each committee.
- Conduct an analysis of the club's **financial information**. What has been happening to your income over the last three years (sponsorship, membership trends)? What is happening to your expenditure over the last three years?
- Conduct an analysis of your **player registration/membership data**. Is adult and junior membership growing or declining over the last three years?
- Conduct an analysis of all the sports programmes you currently run throughout the year: Festivals and tournaments, holiday camps etc.
- Gain an understanding of where your governing body is heading in terms of its strategic plans and priorities; read the national governing body's strategic plan.

What Next?

Once you have collated all this information, meet as a team to identify the key trends, common issues/challenges and key priority areas for the club over the coming years.

SWOT, Stakeholder and Resource Examples

Figures 2.4–2.6 show templates that can be used by your club. Further details on how to complete each section of the plan will be given in this chapter.

SWOT ANALYSIS EXAMPLE

Strengths	Weaknesses	Opportunities	Threats
• Popularity of your sport • Dedicated coaches • Long-serving club administrators	• Poorly-structured youth development • Execution of strategic plan • Volunteers not sufficiently engaged • Financial spending	• Opportunity to improve community relations • Maximize relationship with the local government • Grow sponsorship income	• Interest of other sports for sponsors • Growth of other sports in terms of participation

Figure 2.4 SWOT analysis

STAKEHOLDER ANALYSIS EXAMPLE

Stakeholder or stakeholder group	How the club currently engages and communicates with stakeholders	What is the current relationship like? - Very poor - Poor - Good - Very good	How important is the stakeholder to the club? -Not important -important -Vital	What can be done to improve the relationship over the next 12 months? (3 clear actions)
Sponsors	• Quarterly meetings • Quarterly Ezine • Quarterly Telephone calls	Poor	Vital	• Conduct monthly meetings with the sponsors • Send thank you notes to sponsors for their support • Invite sponsors to your awards evening

Figure 2.5 Stakeholder analysis

RESOURCE ANALYSIS EXAMPLE

Resources	What you have at present	What you need in the future (3–5 years)
Volunteers or staff in the club	8 volunteer board members 10 club coaches	1 part-time youth director
Financial	$2,000 cash in the bank	$15,000 cash in the bank
Infrastructure	1 x Park pitch rented from the local government	Upgrade of the changing rooms
Equipment	Sports equipment (10 balls, 10 bibs and 20 cones)	Sports equipment (200 balls, 200 bibs and 400 cones)

Figure 2.6 Resource analysis

> You can find a blank copy of the "Resource Analysis" template in the appendix.

Doing Your Research: 1:1s and Focus Groups

Research should be conducted with your members, parents, coaches and players. The research will take the form of 1:1s and focus groups.

Questions to ask different key stakeholders regarding the current situation in your club are given below:

Members/Spectators
❖ What are the most important factors for you to attend a live game or event?
❖ Can you rate the overall experience on game day at the club? (1 is very poor, 5 is excellent.)

- ❖ What is the main social media platform you use? Do you visit our website? If yes, how often per week? Rate the content.
- ❖ How well does the club communicate information to you as a club member? How is the club viewed in the local community? What needs improvement?
- ❖ What should the club prioritise in the next two years?

Sponsors
- ❖ Are you satisfied with your sponsorship of the club? If not, why not? What are the most important factors for you to sponsor the club? What does the club do well and what needs improvement?
- ❖ How do you view the club?
- ❖ How is the club viewed in the local community?
- ❖ How well does the club communicate information to you as a sponsor?
- ❖ What should the club prioritise in the next two years?

Players
- ❖ How would you rate the standard of coaching at the club?
- ❖ What does the club need to do to improve the level of coaching? How well does the club communicate information to you as a player?
- ❖ What should the club prioritise in the next two years?

Coaches
- ❖ What is your coaching qualification?
- ❖ How would you rate the standard of coaching at the club?
- ❖ Is there a need for more personal development training and educational courses?
- ❖ What does the club need to do in order to improve the level of coaching? How well does the club communicate information to you as a coach?
- ❖ What should the club prioritise in the next two years?

Parents
- ❖ Is the club a welcoming club?
- ❖ How well does the club communicate information to you as a parent? How would you rate the standard of coaching at the club?
- ❖ What should the club prioritise in the next two years?

Conducting Research
In order to identify where you are at now, the club needs to conduct research which will include the areas outlined below:

1. **Questionnaires:** Online or printed surveys
2. **Focus groups/1: 1:** Deep dive into a subject

3. **Desktop research:** Financial data, membership data, industry reports, articles, online information
4. **Situation analysis:** A situation analysis consists of a SWOT, PEST, stakeholder analysis, competitor analysis, resource analysis

Doing the Research: Gathering Information

Player Registration/Membership Data

Gather information about the club's players/members. Consider the following questions:

- How many players have registered with the club over the last three years? (Broken down by age groups and gender)
- Has membership increased, decreased or remained unchanged over the last three years?
- How does your membership compare with other clubs in your area/across the province in similar catchments?
- What are the population trends in local and surrounding communities?
- What is the retention rate of new and existing members?
- What do you know about people's skills and how to utilise them as potential volunteers within your membership?

Sport Programmes

Gather information about your club's activities. Consider the following questions:

- What do you offer during any given season? (Adult games, youth festivals and tournaments, holiday camps etc.)
- How successful have you been in competitions over the past three years?
- Which activities attract the most support? (Grassroots/youth festivals, adult games etc.)
- How many training sessions do you run each week? (breakdown by age)

Doing the Research: Surveys

Distributing surveys (printed or online) is a great way to gather research for your plan. The surveys should be sent to your stakeholders such as players, coaches, spectators, parents etc.

Typical questions to consider:

- Rate the game day experience. What needs improvement?
- Rate the administration in the club. What needs improvement?
- Rate the coaching/academy/grassroots programmes in the club. What needs improvement?

- How is the club viewed in the local community?
- Rate the facilities at the club. What needs improvement?
- Rate how the club communicates with you. What needs improvement?
- What needs improving in the club over the next two to four years?

Once you have collated and analysed all the information from the 1:1s, focus groups, surveys, data and situational analyses, start to identify the key themes and priorities. The findings from this step should be summarised and included in the research section of your club development plan.

Used with permission from Shutterstock/Tatiana Diuvbanova.

REMEMBER

Talk to all your key stakeholders during the research step (players, coaches, admin volunteers, spectators, sponosrs etc.)

Step 3: Where Do You Want to Be?
This step helps you to identify:

- A clear vision, mission and value statement for your club
- Key goals for the next two to five years
- SMART objectives under each goal

Vision Statement

A vision outlines the ambition of the club. It clearly outlines where you are heading. Your vision should engage all stakeholders, exciting and motivating them to actively support the club in achieving your vision. The vision must be clear and ambitious but realistic.

Use the template below to help you develop a vision for your club:

Vision Example

First, list the words you want to see in the vision statement:

1. Premier grassroots clubs in our region
2. Known for developing great talent etc.

Now complete the sentences below:

In 20xx, our club will be …
By 20xx, we want …
By 20xx, we will have …

> You can find a blank copy of the "Vision Statement" template in the appendix.

THINK!

Vision statement: In one sentence, it describes a clear and inspirational long-term ambition or dream.

It's your north star!

Process for Developing Your Vision

The following processes should be adopted when developing your vision:	☑
Set up a workshop with the board and key individuals from the club. It would be of benefit to have an external facilitator to run the workshop.	☐
Depending on the number of people, split into small groups. Ask each group to develop the front page of their local newspaper in two to five years' time (whatever the term of your strategic plan). Develop the heading in the newspaper, the articles on the homepage and photo about your club – what does the front page say about your club?	☐
Within your group, write down the key words you want to see in your vision on small pieces of paper (i.e. A5 card). Display on the floor and debate.	☐

- As a combined group, select the key words that must be in the new vision statement. ☐
- Start to create a vision statement (one sentence) in terms of your future state. Identify a date when this vision is to be realised. For example, 31 December 202x. ☐
- Take a break, then ask the board to review the vision statement within seven days. ☐
- Ensure that the board confirms the vision statement. ☐

Mission Statement

The mission simply describes your clubs purpose and reason for existence: What you do, for whom, and what the benefits are.

It ensures that everyone is on the same page as to why your club exists and what it does, while clarifying your role and activities with the stakeholders (i.e. sponsors, membership, etc).

THINK!

Mission statement: A one-sentence statement describing the reason for an organisation to exist.

Use the template below to help you develop a mission for your club:

Mission Example

What do we do today?	Organise volleyball games and develop players (both adults and youth) to play and enjoy the game
How do we do it?	By providing great coaching, great facilities and great organisation of activities
For whom do we do it?	Players, parents, coaches, members and spectators
What is the benefit?	To be an integral part of the local community, help to improve health and community spirit
Draft club mission	To develop Crumlin United Volleyball Club as the hub of the community and to develop volleyball in the local area at youth and senior level

> You can find a blank copy of the "Mission Statement" template in the appendix.

Process for Developing Your Mission

The following processes should be adopted when developing your mission:	☑
Set up a workshop with the board and key individuals from the club. It would be of benefit to have an external facilitator to run the workshop.	☐
Depending on the number of people, split into small groups. Ask each group to answer the following questions: ❖ Why do we exist? ❖ What is the purpose of our club? ❖ Who are we running the club for and why?	☐
Within your group, write down the key words you want to see in your mission on A5 card. Display on the floor and debate.	☐
As a combined group, select the key words.	☐
Start to create a mission statement (one sentence) in terms of the purpose of your club.	☐
Take a break, then ask the board to review within seven days.	☐
Ensure that the board confirms the mission statement.	☐

Values

Values outline how you will behave as a club to your various stakeholders. Values are a set the core beliefs held by a sports organisation. When a sports club core values are clear and genuine, they differentiate the organisation from others, making it stand out. This not only helps in attracting players, fans, funders and sponsors but also in fostering loyalty, as people tend to stick with clubs that they feel understand and represent them. Everyone in the club must understand that the values are really important to the organisation and must be adhered to by those associated with the club. Finally, clubs must ensure they recruit volunteers, coaches and players who demonstrate these core values.

Use this following template to help you develop values for your club.

Values Example

Core values   *Values definition*

Fair play — We compete with integrity and respect. We follow the rules, honour the spirit of the game and treat opponents, officials and teammates with dignity – win or lose.

Accountability — We take ownership of our actions and decisions. We hold ourselves and each other to high standards, admit mistakes and learn from them. We show up prepared, reliable and committed to our responsibilities.

Excellence — We strive for the best in everything we do – on the field, in the club and in the community. Through discipline, passion and a growth mindset, we aim to raise the bar and set new standards of performance and professionalism.

Teamwork — We succeed together. We value every role, share responsibility and support each other on and off the field.

(Value definitions are the detailed explanations or descriptions of each individual core value of the club. A good value definition should be clear, memorable and actionable.)

> You can find a blank copy of the "Values Development" template in the appendix.

THINK!

Consider placing your values in your changing room or clubhouse.

In addition, ensure you recruit staff/volunteers who share the same values as the clubs.

Process for Developing Your Values

The following processes should be adopted when developing your values:	☑
Set up a workshop with the board and key individuals from the club. It would be of benefit to have an external facilitator to run the workshop.	☐
Depending on the number of people, split into small groups.	☐
Within your group, write down the values you want to see in your club on A5 card (consider what behaviours do you value? What behaviours are unacceptable?) Display on the floor and debate.	☐

As a combined group, select the key values. It is recommended you to select between three and five core values.	☐
Start to create a definition for each value selected.	☐
Take a break, then ask the board to review within seven days.	☐
Ensure that the board confirms the value definition.	☐

Goals

Goals are the key priorities you need to focus on to fulfil your vision. Goals are broad areas of focus and the findings from your *research* and *vision* statement will be taken into consideration.

Questions to ask:

❖ What are the key themes or priorities that came up time and time again during the research?
❖ What key areas must we focus on to achieve our vision?

Potential Goals to Consider

(Write down on A5 cards when running your goals' workshop):

- STRENGTHEN GOVERNANCE
- DEVELOP THE YOUTH (MALE & FEMALE)
- IMPROVE ADMINISTRATION
- GROW INCOME GENERATION
- STRENGTHEN FINANCIAL MANAGEMENT
- IMPROVE COACHING/EDUCATION (MALE & FEMALE)
- SENIOR TEAM DEVELOPMENT (MALE & FEMALE)
- GROW VOLUNTEER RECRUITMENT
- DEVELOP & MAINTAIN THE FACILITY
- GROW MEMBERSHIP RECRUITMENT AND RETENTION
- LEAD ON COMMUNITY DEVELOPMENT/ LINKS
- OTHERS – FEEL FREE TO ADD OTHER GOALS

Process for Developing Your Goals

The following processes should be adopted when developing your **goals:**	✓
Set up a workshop with the board and key individuals from the club. It would be of benefit to have an external facilitator to run the workshop.	☐
Depending on the number of people, split into small groups. Present the findings from the research and display the vision statement.	☐
Write down the broad goals in the list below on A5 card (please add in other as you see fit) – one goal per card.	☐
Ask your group to select four or five goals (the broad goals should be selected based on the research and vision).	☐
Take a break, then ask the board to review within seven days.	☐
Ensure that the board confirms the four or five goals.	☐
Once you have selected the goals, identify one person on the club's board to lead on each goal, i.e. strengthening governance could be the responsibility of the Chair of the board.	☐

Used with permission from Shutterstock/Ground Picture.

REMEMBER

If you want to make sure goals are met, assign a board member to an individual goal.

SMART Objectives
What are your SMART objectives under each goal?

Specific, Measureable, Achieveable, Responsibility Time-Bound

Once you have analysed where things currently stand and have decided on the club's goals for the future, the next step is to develop objectives for each goal. The objectives must be realistic in terms of time scale, cost and resources. The objectives should link to the findings obtained during your research. Each objective must be measurable with an owner and a clear timeline.

Objectives can be presented using the example template shown in Figure 2.7.

TEMPLATE
STRATEGIC GOAL: DEVELOP YOUR YOUTH PROGRAM

Objective	Key Actions (list key tasks under each objective)	Completion Date	Responsibility (who is the owner)	KPI/Measure (Target / Measurement)	WRAG (is it on schedule)
Appoint a youth/junior director (voluntary role)	• Develop Job Description • Hold interviews and recruit. Select person • etc	31 July 202x	Chair	Youth/junior director appointed	🟢
Develop coaching curriculum for the club	• Hold workshop with coaches • Develop curriculum for various age groups • email document to all coaches and set up training sessions • etc	30 September 202x	Youth / Junior Director	Curriculum developed. Booklet printed	🟢
Organise 2 coach-education workshops per year	• Discuss and agree 2 workshops per year • Secure speaker and venue • Promote to the coaches • Run the workshops • etc	31 October 202x	Youth / Junior Director	2 workshops held per years	🟢

Progress/Outcome Key - RAG: ☐ Not started, no action required ■ In progress and on track ■ In progress, some action required ■ Significant action required ■ Completed

Figure 2.7 Strategic objectives template

You can find a blank copy of the "SMART Objectives" template in the appendix.

Once all the objectives have been defined under each goal, these will be presented to the board for final approval.

Process for Developing Your Objectives

The following processes should be adopted when developing your smart objectives:	☑
Write down the broad goals, selected from your previous workshop, on A5 card (please add others as you see fit) – one goal per card.	☐
Ask your group to create two to five objectives under each goal. The objectives must have an owner, delivery date and clear KPI or measurement.	☐
Once you have selected the objectives, ensure the board member responsible for the goal is fully aware of the objectives.	☐
Add the objectives to the template provided (refer to the "SMART Objectives" template in the appendix). Also outline the top seven to ten actions required to ensure that the objective is achieved and the resources (human or financial) required.	☐

TO DO!

Following board approval, it is recommended that the draft plan is sent to your coaches, members, players and sponsors to gain their feedback. The purpose of doing this is to gain their buy-in, obtain feedback and to identify any unforeseen objectives.

Step 4: How Do You Get There?

Action Plans

Action plans are developed for each objective.

Action plans should be detailed and highlight the key actions or tasks required in order to achieve the objective. The actions should be prioritised by timeline.

A good 'rule of thumb' is having between seven and ten tasks or actions under each objective.

These actions should be inserted into the objectives template.

By involving your staff or volunteers in developing the action plans. This will further entrench them as contributors and ultimately motivate them to take a more active role in the pursuit of the club's vision, goals and objectives.

The principles of SMART are also valid when completing your action plans.

Budgeting

It is important to develop an annual budget for your plan. This will include all the income and expenditure for a given year.

Having developed your plan, it is now an important task to develop a budget against each objective together with the normal costs associated with running a club, i.e. insurance, rent, electricity etc.

By incorporating the budget process into the strategic planning process, your club can begin to ascertain the financial impact of the goals and objectives and the implementation.

Equally as important, the budget process will identify whether your club will have sufficient revenues to implement all planned activities, and if not, has an opportunity to consider strategies to generate more funds or to consider eliminating some planned activities which they will not have funds to implement.

Over the course of implementing the clubs plan, the finance team or committee must continually monitor the budget to assess financial performance against forecasts and for cash-flow management purposes (see Figure 2.8).

BUDGET TEMPLATE													
Insert club name													
Month	1	2	3	4	5	6	7	8	9	10	11	12	Total
Income	0	0	0	0	0	0	0	0	0	0	0	0	0
Expenditure	0	0	0	0	0	0	0	0	0	0	0	0	0
Gross profit	0	0	0	0	0	0	0	0	0	0	0	0	0
Expenses/overheads	1	2	3	4	5	6	7	8	9	10	11	12	Total
Premises (rent, rates)	0	0	0	0	0	0	0	0	0	0	0	0	0
Power (light, heat, electricity, gas)	0	0	0	0	0	0	0	0	0	0	0	0	0
Telephone	0	0	0	0	0	0	0	0	0	0	0	0	0
Insurance	0	0	0	0	0	0	0	0	0	0	0	0	0
Postage and carriage	0	0	0	0	0	0	0	0	0	0	0	0	0
Advertising	0	0	0	0	0	0	0	0	0	0	0	0	0
Interest and bank charges payable	0	0	0	0	0	0	0	0	0	0	0	0	0
Stationery	0	0	0	0	0	0	0	0	0	0	0	0	0
Drawings, wages or salaries	0	0	0	0	0	0	0	0	0	0	0	0	0
Sports Equipment	0	0	0	0	0	0	0	0	0	0	0	0	0
Motor expenses (Mileage)	0	0	0	0	0	0	0	0	0	0	0	0	0
Accountancy fees	0	0	0	0	0	0	0	0	0	0	0	0	0
Legal/professional fees	0	0	0	0	0	0	0	0	0	0	0	0	0
Total expenses/overheads	0	0	0	0	0	0	0	0	0	0	0	0	0
Income	1	2	3	4	5	6	7	8	9	10	11	12	Total
Ticketing	0	0	0	0	0	0	0	0	0	0	0	0	0
Sponsorship	0	0	0	0	0	0	0	0	0	0	0	0	0
Government Grants	0	0	0	0	0	0	0	0	0	0	0	0	0
Food and Beverages	0	0	0	0	0	0	0	0	0	0	0	0	0
Merchandising	0	0	0	0	0	0	0	0	0	0	0	0	0
Advertising	0	0	0	0	0	0	0	0	0	0	0	0	0
Other	0	0	0	0	0	0	0	0	0	0	0	0	0
Total Income	0	0	0	0	0	0	0	0	0	0	0	0	0
PROFIT	0	0	0	0	0	0	0	0	0	0	0	0	0

Figure 2.8 Budget template

Process for Developing Your Budget

The following processes should be adopted when developing your budget: ☑

Bring together a team to look at the annual finances (set up a finance committee).	☐
Create a budget – use the template on the previous page.	☐
Confirm all costs and potential income across the whole club (consider costs linked to the goals and objectives, as well as monthly operational costs, such as electricity, telephone etc.). Consider all income such as membership fees, sponsorship, event income, grants etc.	☐
Update budget sheet based on the information supplied and include a small contingency of 10 per cent.	☐
Agree budget with the board (the aim is to make profit each year). This should be approved by the board one month before the start of the next financial year.	☐
Ensure that the committees and various departments that spend money are sent a copy of the annual budget, with clear levels of spend attached (delegated levels of expenditure).	☐
Finance committee to produce monthly or quarterly actuals versus budget and to ensure that the club is keeping to the financials. This report should be sent to the board.	☐

Organisational Chart

It is important to align your structure to the club's plan. Aligning an organisational chart to the club plan ensures the structure supports the organisational goals or areas of priority.

Look at the goals and align them to your club structure – for many grassroots clubs, this may be committees that operate under the board. It is recommended that your club has the following structure and sub-committees in place:

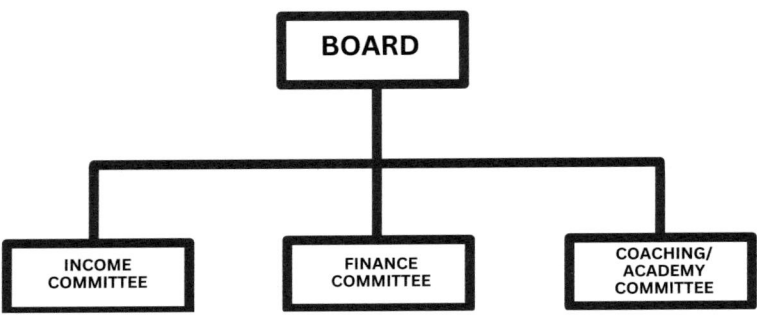

Used with permission from Shutterstock/William Edge.

Process for Developing Your Organisational Chart

The following processes should be adopted when developing your organisational chart:	☑
Bring together a team to look at the organisational structure in order to deliver on the strategic plan and to ensure the week to week operational aspects are actioned. In addition, look at the current roles and determine if they are aligned with the club's plan. Identify redundant positions.	☐
Look at the key strategic goals and match them against your organisational structure i.e. goals (Academy development = Academy committee, Income generation = Income generation committee etc.).	☐
Create an organisational chart – refer to the example shown in the above section of Organisational chart. Avoid overly complex hierarchies that slow decision making.	☐
Identify the key personnel required to be part of each committee or role in the club. Ensure no individual is overburdened.	☐
Develop job description and KPIs for each role outlined in the organisational chart. Ensure each position has the signed authority to execute the plan.	☐
Agree organisational chart with the board.	☐
Ensure that the various committees report directly to the board each month and that the various staff members communicate with each other on a weekly basis. Good communication across the club is critical.	☐

Step 5: Writing Your Plan

Writing Your Development Plan

It is time to complete the 'internal' club development plan (refer to the appendix). This plan is for internal use only.

The final step in the planning process is to write up an external plan using the information produced from steps 1–4. This external facing document should include high-quality images of players, coaches and members, and it will be shared with the various stakeholders.

The production of an external document is not an essential requirement. A club does not have to complete this stage, although it is the best practice and will provide your club with a tool to communicate with your key stakeholders, such as the government, sponsors, funders, etc.

The main differences between the internal and external plans are as follows:

INTERNAL PLAN	EXTERNAL PLAN
For internal use only	For external use only
Will be used to monitor the implementation of the plan throughout the year.	Aimed at your public facing stakeholders, such as your sponsors, government, local community organisations etc.

Ideally, your external plan should include:

- A message from your chair
- A review of the current position and 'health' of the club
- A statement of your new 'vision', mission and values of the club
- An outline of the key goals
- An outline of the objectives
- An outline of the resources and finances required (this will also include the committee structure)

Launching Your Plan

Once you have created your plan, an event should be organised to officially launch the document to all your key stakeholders.

The launch of an external document is not an essential requirement. A club does not have to complete this stage, although it is the best practice and will provide your club with a tool to communicate with your key stakeholders such as government, sponsors and funders as well as generate positive media exposure for your organisation.

Process for Launching Your Plan

The following processes should be adopted when launching your club development plan: ☑

Board to agree a date and location to launch the club development plan ☐

Board to invite key stakeholders including, but not limited to: ☐

a. Board members
b. Committee members
c. Players
d. Coaches
e. Local sponsors and business people
f. Politicians
g. Local community organisations
h. Members of the media

Develop an agenda for the event. For example: ☐

- Welcome by the chair
- Speech by the local mayor or dignitary
- An outline of the new vision, mission, values, goals and key objectives
- Photo opportunities

Develop a press release for the launch event and plan. This should be given to all local media after the event. The press release should be accompanied by photographs from the event. ☐

Upload the press release onto your website and social media platforms. ☐

Send copies of the plan via email or by post to your key stakeholders and local community organisations. ☐

Step 6: Measuring Your Success

How Do You Know If You Are Succeeding?

Regular monitoring of your plan is essential to ensure that progress towards achieving your goals, objectives and overall vision is being made.

This is often a step that many clubs overlook following the development of their plan, yet it is fundamental.

It is recommended for the board to review the goals and objectives every *quarter* at its regular meetings.

The WRAG column is used to update the progress of the objectives in terms of delivery and fulfilment. The objective owner should update this table with a few words on the current situation of their specific objective (see Figure 2.9). In addition, this column should be colour-coded – **white, red, amber or green**.

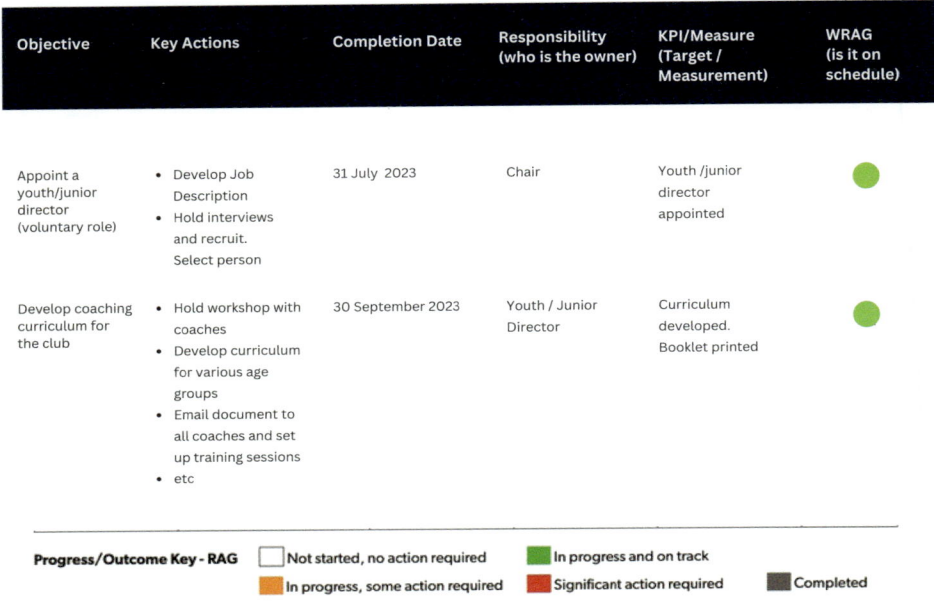

Figure 2.9 Strategic objectives template

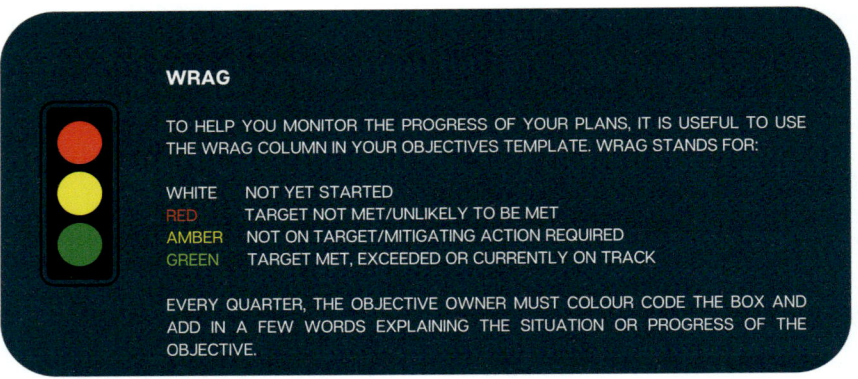

Reviewing the Plan

The board should ask the following questions each quarter when reviewing the plan:

❖ Are the objectives and action plans being achieved on time and on target? If not, why not?
❖ Based on current progress, will the objectives and action plans be achieved within the set timeframe? If not, why?

- Should new action plans be considered and developed to achieve objectives?
- Should we allocate a new person to be responsible for completing the objective and action plans?
- Does the responsible person have the appropriate resources to achieve the objectives and action plans?
- Are we on target budget-wise?

What Happens at the End of Your Club Plan?

Once you have reached the end of your plan's timeframe, you should start the process again by conducting new research, setting up the various workshops to identify your goals and objectives for the years ahead. One slight difference is that you may not need to spend the same amount of time defining your vision, mission and values. It may be a case of simply reconfirming the vision, mission and values.

Final Thought

This chapter, focused on creating a comprehensive club plan through a step-by-step process. This involved conducting research, defining your vision, mission, values and setting clear goals and objectives. We also highlighted the importance of establishing a budget and organizational structure, along with the need for ongoing monitoring of the plan's progress. The next step for your club is to meet, review this chapter and begin developing your plan. Now that you have a plan, the next step is to ensure you provide a great experience at your club.

Used with permission from Shutterstock/Master1305.

3

Club Experience
Offering the best experience at your club

Grassroots sports clubs must be committed to providing an exceptional experience for every member and guest, ensuring that everyone feels welcomed. The club should be dedicated to making every visit rewarding and enjoyable.

> In this chapter you will learn:
>
> 1. How to be a welcoming club
> 2. Areas to consider in order to improve the experience
> 3. How to recruit and retain players/members

Recruiting good staff and volunteers, combined with clear and consistent communication (see Chapter 8) and deep community integration (see Chapter 7) are essential for ensuring your club provides a high-quality experience for everyone involved – from players and coaches to members, parents and volunteers. Having great staff and volunteers, consistent and clear communication (refer to Chapter 8) alongside being integrated into your community (refer to Chapter 7), are vital areas to ensure your club delivers a quality experience for all those involved, from players and coaches to members, club volunteers and parents.

> Priority areas to adopt in your club after reading this chapter:
>
> 1. Conduct research on your game day or tournament experience; identify areas of possible improvement
> 2. Improve communication within the club – to players, volunteers, coaches and parents

Be a Welcoming Club

Having a friendly, welcoming and sociable club is an extremely important factor for a successful grassroots club.

DOI: 10.4324/9781003650362-4

It is vital to get the basics right. This means you must be a welcoming club for existing members, parents, players, away teams and spectators and new members, coaches and players.

Why is this important?

- Players, parents and coaches will want to join a club with a welcoming ethos.
- Parents will be happy to send their kids to play in a club whose staff will look after their children from day one.
- A positive experience at the club will help you to retain your current players and members.

Before the visit of a new member or player, you should ensure that the following information is on your website:

- Information on training nights
- How to get to the club venue
- Membership information
- Key welcome information for new members and players; key contacts in the club, policies

During the first visit, you should:

- Introduce the new member to the coach and other relevant people.
- Explain club regulations and policies, such as code of conduct for members.
- Explain the registration process – completing forms, making payments etc.

After the first visit of a new player, member or coach, you should:

- Send a welcome email or text to the player, member or parent of the youth within one week of joining.
- Ask the new members to connect to your club's social media channels, WhatsApp groups or other club messaging app groups.

Welcoming New Members/Players: Checklist

Before Their First Visit

- Send the important club information to the new member or player via text or email, including how to get to the club, training session times and access the club premises.
- Email or text the club membership information and registration forms.
- Call or email to ask questions about any special needs, support and check if they have questions.
- Inform the coach and other people involved in welcoming new players.

During Their First Visit

- Introduce the new players to the coach and other relevant people.
- Provide a tour of the club premises and facilities.
- Welcome the new player to the squad before the first training session, game or activity.
- Sit with the member and address any special needs, support and check if they have questions.
- Explain the club's culture and expectations of members and players.
- Explain club regulations and policies – code of conduct, safeguarding etc.
- Explain the registration process – completing forms, making payments etc.

After Their First Visit

- Coach to follow up within one week – ask how the first visit went and address any reasonable requirements they may have.
- Assist them with the registration and payment process if needed.
- On the second visit, ensure someone they met on the first visit is there to greet them.
- Introduce them to other members including any club leaders.
- In the case of disability, put any agreed adaptations, modifications or supports in place to enable full participation.
- Before the member or player leaves, ask how things went and address any issues.
- Tell the member or player they are valued and you look forward to seeing them next time.

Indicators of a Positive Club Culture

Some indicators of club culture can be:

- Having a 'winning isn't everything' mentality
- Whether all coaches have a basic qualification
- That all coaches have completed a club induction
- The social programme in the club
- The agreed transition steps for underage to adult team training/environment
- The agreed minimum number of games per age group
- Having a policy of 'equal play' in children's fun games
- The number of women and minorities involved as coaches or in committees

TIP

Brainstorm with other club members about what your club culture is, discussing why and where you want to make improvements.

Figure 3.1 shows six ways to create a welcoming culture.

SIX WAYS TO CREATE A WELCOMING CULTURE

STEP 1: DEFINE THE CLUB'S VISION, CULTURE AND VALUES

Is the club focussed on maximising participation, sporting performance or both? Ensure that you communicate the vision to all involved at the earliest opportunity. If people new to the club know what the club is about from the start, they will fit in better as it avoids surprises later on. Define and communicate the clubs values to current and new members, players, coaches and parents. Finally, develop the right culture in the club that is welcoming & friendly.

STEP 2: MAKE PEOPLE FEEL SAFE

Create a physically safe, non-threatening environment for all members, whether they are children or adults. Coaches and board members play an important role in making people feel safe. Coaches should be aware of how to speak to young players and to be aware of any signs of bullying.

STEP 3: MAKE PEOPLE FEEL LIKE THEY BELONG

Create a strong sense of inclusion and belonging, and ensure there is a specific club style that welcomes and integrates new players, members and supporters.

STEP 4: COMMUNICATE WELL

Have a strong communication strategy so that club stakeholders are continually informed and empowered with information. Ensure dialogue is two-way. This may include regular meetings with members, parents, coaches and players, as well as setting up messenger groups for regular information exchange.

STEP 5: RECOGNISE INDIVIDUALS

Have a strategy for the club to develop and recognise its people not just as sports people but also as individuals who contribute to their club and the broader community.

STEP 6: GET BUY IN AND UNDERSTANDING

Ensure that all members understand why the club culture is so important and what their role is in upholding the club's vision and values. Train staff and volunteers to be approachable, courteous, and supportive. Encourage a friendly attitude and a willingness to assist members, players, parents, coaches and visitors.

Figure 3.1 Six ways to create a welcoming culture

Improving the Experience

Create a Club Brochure

A club brochure is a great way to provide relevant information to new and existing members. The club brochure sets out the values, history, list of policies and expectations of all the members (including code of conducts), useful contact numbers and a general overview of how things are done. This document does not need to be a book: Three or four pages would suffice.

It could include a selection of topics from the following:

- Welcome from the president/Chair
- Club contacts
- Club history
- Club values
- Key dates and social functions
- Information nights
- Coaching style and 'way of play'
- Membership fee/packages
- Codes of conduct and club policies
- Working with children – conducting safeguarding checks
- Club rules

Clean and Tidy Club Spaces, Facilities and Buildings

Nobody likes to attend a facility that is not clean and tidy. This sends out a negative message to anyone who uses or visits your facility.

Well-maintained venues project an image of professionalism.

What does this include?

- Ensuring that seats in stands are cleaned regularly
- Ensuring that no rubbish is left in the stands or at pitch side
- Ensuring that the clubhouse is cleaned weekly; toilets, bar and carpets should be deep cleaned regularly
- Ensuring that all rubbish, i.e. plastic water bottles, are removed and put in the bin after training sessions
- Ensuring a smoke-free environment at the club
- Keeping equipment clean and presentable

Used with permission from Shutterstock/Jacob Lund.

Improving the Game Day/Tournament Experience (Fans/Spectators)

Anyone attending a game or tournament at your club should have a positive experience. This will result in more people attending your home games and potentially increase revenue from sales of food, beverages etc.

Your club must conduct research on the current experience and then introduce new ways to improve the overall enjoyment for parents, spectators, members, coaches and visiting clubs.

Research can include:

- ❖ Understanding why people come to your events
- ❖ Walking in the shoes of the spectator – from parking the car to entering the venue to pre-game entertainment to leaving the venue
- ❖ Conducting a focus group, as well as online surveys, with members, players, parents and coaches on the current experience, identifying ways in which it can be improved

Following the research, the club should collate the findings by completing this template:

WHAT DID THE RESEARCH TELL US ABOUT THE GAME-DAY EXPERIENCE?

Areas We Do Well (and Must Continue to Do Well)

1. We have two stewards who make everyone feel welcome as they enter the venue.
2. Our food offering is excellent. We source all our food locally and feedback has been excellent.
3. The facilities outside the club house are well-maintained and clean.

Areas to Improve

1. Additional stewards in the car park is required. Cars are not parked in a way that maximises the space.
2. We need to clean the carpet in the bar area in our clubhouse.
3. We need additional volunteers to help on our game-day posts on social media.

Outline Five Actions That Will Help to Improve the Game-day Experience

1. Appoint two new volunteers for game-day posts on social media.
2. Appoint two new stewards to the car park. Create a parking plan to maximise the space.
3. Ask the local carpet company to clean the carpet in the bar.
4. Provide useful information on our website such as bus and train timetables on game days.
5. Conduct a monthly 'clean up' around the club house.

You can find a blank copy of the "Game-Day Experience" template in the appendix.

The following provides a list of areas which could be considered during this process:

- Improve the quality of the food.
- Have helpful & enthusiastic marshals/stewards. Give them some basic training on how to welcome people to the venue.
- Organise events for the family.
- Ensure the club has all the necessary information on your digital channels/social media regarding game-day times and kick off, giving details of where to park.
- Ensure that there is an 'abuse-free' environment and a proactive policy to address offenders.

Recruit and Retain Brilliant Stewards (Marshals)

Designated ground stewards can help teams on game day. They provide a direct and ongoing interaction between your club and spectators. The main duties of a steward are to:

- Represent the club as a first point-of-contact for emergencies and urgent event issues
- Present a positive public face to those in attendance
- To assist with the circulation of spectators
- To prevent overcrowding
- To provide overall safety and security during the event
- To provide information to spectators and attendees

Stewards are particularly important in semi-professional or professional clubs, but that is not to say that a community club should not introduce this concept for locally organised events.

They assist in ensuring that all attendees are kept safe and well throughout the game. Ground stewards should be easily identifiable and help with the day-to-day experience of all those who attend a ground on game day.

The Role of Voluntary Stewards on Event Days

A marshal's role is to maintain a safe and secure environment in their given area, ensuring that any breach of the following regulations is brought to a safe conclusion.

- Crowd control – sideline duty
- Customer care – usher and assist patrons, give disability awareness assistance, direct patrons to designated smoking areas
- Emergency procedures – e.g. assisting with facility evacuation

Stewards are normally not paid in monetary terms. However, there are other incentives for stewards, such as a free meal and beverage on a game or tournament day. A training course should be provided for all stewards.

Used with permission from Shutterstock/Kostiantyn Voitenko.

Requirements to be a Steward
- Over 18 years of age
- Available to work at weekends and some week nights
- Fit and active
- Friendly
- Courteous
- Enthusiastic

Create the Right Environment in Terms of Respect and Responsibility

Creating the right environment for your players is vital. Everyone must play a part in creating an enjoyable, safe and inclusive environment.

The respect codes of conduct are in place to ensure that everyone involved within a sports association, league or club is playing their part to give the players a positive experience.

Respect the Code of Conduct for Spectators, Parents and Coaches

Respect is the collective responsibility of everyone involved in sport, at all levels, to create a fair, safe and enjoyable game environment. It is the behavioural code for sport.

All the staff and volunteers are responsible for promoting high standards of behaviour in the game.

The conduct of players and spectators can have a big impact on how your club is viewed/perceived by other clubs, and their supporters, as well as the general public. A lack of respect shown on the pitch to opponents and referees, for example, will negatively impact the club's image and the work of your club's marketing/branding team.

Introducing a respect program in your club will be important when looking to improve the overall experience. The following steps outline practical ways to improve behaviour, both on the pitch and on the sidelines (see Figure 3.2).

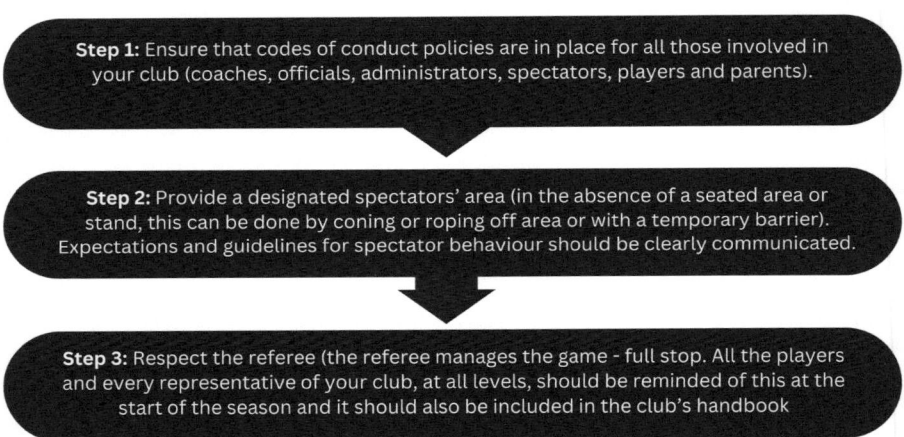

Figure 3.2 Steps to improve behaviour

You can find a blank copy of the "Code of Conducts" in the appendix.

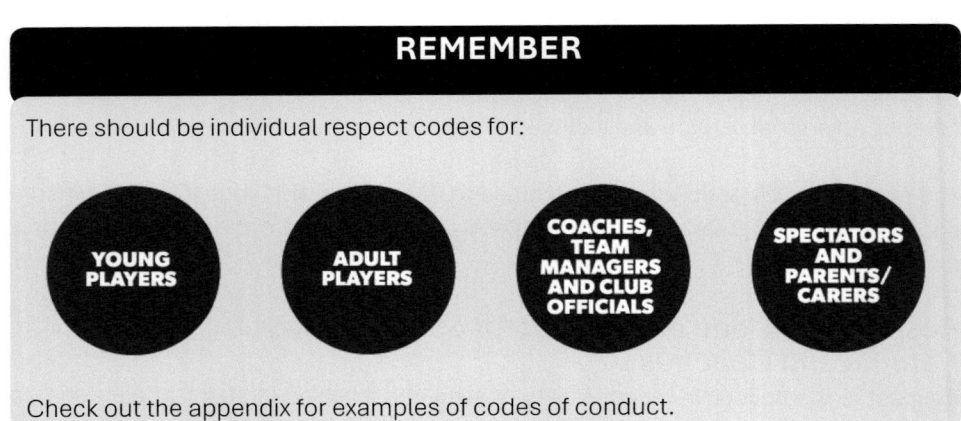

Check out the appendix for examples of codes of conduct.

Used with permission from Shutterstock/Dmitry Molchanov.

Communication with Parents of Youth Players

It is important to maintain regular communication with parents. After all they know their children best. This can be achieved by:

❖ Holding an open day for all underage players and their families
❖ Presenting the training philosophy and 'way of play' at the start of the season
❖ Presenting the code of conduct to the underage players and parents
❖ Outlining the behaviour expected of the younger members and parents during training and game days
❖ Explaining the membership fees for the season
❖ Holding regular 1:1s between coaches and parents throughout the season

Use the following tools when communicating with parents:

Tips to Consider When Engaging Parents

1. Remain calm during conversations with parents. Ensure you have considered the key points you want to get across when meeting a parent.
2. Make sure you have strong communication between the coaching team and the parents. Use the various communication methods outlined above during the season.
3. If their child has not been selected for the next game or is getting limited game time, approach the parent and explain your decision. It is important to be honest and to proactively engage with the parents outlining your reasons for your decision. It is also important to involve the parents in the development of their child. This can be done by asking them to get involved in areas to improve their son or daughter's performance.
4. Communicate your 'style of play' to the parents at the start of the season. This will ensure parents are aware of the style of play and will hopefully restrict from a different style of play during a game.

Used with permission from Shutterstock/Gorodenkoff.

TIP

Approach your local school to get kids interested in attending a youth session at your club.

REMEMBER

Set up a WhatsApp group for parents to improve communication.

Linkage between the Underage and Adult Teams
It is important to ensure strong links between the youth and adult teams in a grassroots club. This can be achieved through:

- Regular meetings between the coaching staff of the youth and adult teams
- Inviting younger club members to act as mascots at adult games
- Inviting younger club members to attend adult games
- Asking adult players to attend youth games or training sessions
- Providing older youth team players the opportunity to train or play in the adult teams

Build a Strong Team Spirit in the Club
Everyone likes to be in a community with a strong team spirit. This is equally important when considering the overall experience at your club.

Team spirit in a club environment can boost player/member happiness and retention. Investing time and effort into building a strong team spirit in your club should more than pay off.

Good team spirit will naturally occur where there is a healthy club environment, with players, members and volunteers being treated as valuable people who are involved in setting the values of the club and where open communication is encouraged.

THINK
Organise social events to help members and players connect (e.g. team get-together, family fun days).

THINK
Provide spaces where members, players and coaches can gather, relax and get to know each other.

Ten Tips for Building a Strong Team Spirit
1. Recruit players with a right personality, i.e. no trouble makers.
2. Organise regular team events or nights out. The aim of these events is to strengthen team cohesion outside the normal sporting environment.
3. Have a set of values clearly defined for all players. The way to behave!

4. Organise pre-season and end-of-season trips.
5. Ensure that weekly training sessions are fun and enjoyable as well as educational.
6. Meet early before kick off on game days to build team cohesion.
7. Communicate regularly with all team members, backroom staff and various committee members. When building a strong team spirit, it is important to keep everyone in the loop.
8. Remember that every volunteer, member, player and coach is different. Identify common values to unite everyone.
9. Set a shared vision, mission, values, goals and objectives as a club (see Chapter 2). Communal decision-making is a key element in building team spirit.
10. Take time to celebrate your success. This might be in securing a local sponsor, winning four games in a row or organising a community tournament. Whatever it is, make sure you celebrate and say thanks to those involved.

Used with permission from Shutterstock/dotshock.

REMEMBER

Maintaining a strong team spirit will be a key component during the season.

Used with permission from Shutterstock/KOTOIMAGES.

TIP
The easiest way to recruit new members to a club is to involve current members who can recruit on the club's behalf!

Ensure Your Club Employs the Principles of Inclusion and Diversity

Inclusion essentially means people have a sense of belonging and comfort when being part of something they value; diversity means being aware of, accommodating and celebrating difference. Inclusion and diversity in many ways go hand-in-hand. Real inclusion reflects diversity, i.e. it aims to offer a sense of belonging to everyone, irrespective of gender, marital status, family status, sexual orientation, religion, age, race or ethnicity, and/or disability.

Inclusion and diversity at club level means the conscious development of inclusive principles, policies and programs for all identified minority groups.

Used with permission from Shutterstock/Jacob Lund.

Tips for Becoming an Inclusive Club

❖ Encourage discussion by the board about what inclusivity could mean for your club. Learn more about the principles of inclusion, equality and diversity and what they could mean for your club.
❖ Discuss with other clubs and learn what is working elsewhere.
❖ Identify an inclusive club champion/inclusion officer, who can become a spokesperson for inclusion and drive positive change in your club.
❖ Form a working group to actively champion your club's efforts to become more inclusive. Encourage members to become engaged and put ideas forward.
❖ Research similar membership organisations outside of sport in your locality. What are they doing in terms of inclusion and diversity?
❖ Seek out and invite local community group representation to visit the club, discuss the club's inclusivity plans and provide feedback.
❖ Be willing and open to listen to both the positive and negative feedback about the club's current culture and approach to inclusion, equality and diversity.
❖ Help to develop your own inclusive club plan, encourage everyone in your club to contribute to its development and take ownership of its roll-out.

How to Recruit New Players/Members

People are sometimes hard to motivate. If you're a leader of a grassroots club seeing diminishing participation in activities overall, you're probably looking for ways to give your club a boost. If current member interest fades, chances are likely that your overall membership numbers will decline – and garnering new members will also prove difficult. Soon, the very existence of your club will be in jeopardy.

Here are some strategies to help recruit new players/members to your club:

Advertise and Promote
The first and easiest way to grow your membership/players is by advertising such as;

Website
In almost any club, there will be a member who can create a website, or perhaps a member with a technically-minded family member who can help.

Today, many tools and options are available online for website creation, so nearly anyone can build a simple page. Ensure the club's name is prominently featured on the home page (and elsewhere) and that a contact form or email address is easily found. 'About the club' information is also highly recommended.

Social Media
Make sure you are posting regular content that is engaging and interesting. Clubs should be on the main social platforms. Consider setting up a social media team that will post content based on your club's personality. This could be entertaining, welcoming, community-focused content. The club should use social media to reach new players and members each year. This might include promotion of an open session at various age groups, the request for new coaches or the need for new volunteers at the club.

Local Opportunities
You should be able to find various ways to promote your club and its activities through local and regional websites and other media; typically, these are free (or offered at minimal cost). Check out the 'calendar' sections on local community newspaper sites and make sure your club is listed on your association or league websites.

Use Current Members/Players
The best advertising is word-of-mouth, and the most readily available cheerleaders for your group are your current members/players. Make sure that you continually coach your current members/players to care for the future of the club by cultivating new members/players.

PLAYER RECRUITMENT

Recruitment of players will depend largely on the league you play in. For grassroots sports clubs, this may include:

- Identifying suitable players in lower leagues
- Identifying suitable players in the same league
- Identifying suitable players in higher leagues (both established and fringe players)
- Developing youth players within your youth structures

Comfortable Welcome

During their first club session, ensure you do not embarrass new members/players by asking too much of them immediately. Well-coached players should comfortably introduce themselves to unfamiliar faces. Make sure everyone knows how important it is to make visitors feel welcome and comfortable.

Keep It Fun and Easy to Engage

The most important strategy when it comes to ensuring that your club attracts new members/players is to make it easy to learn about your group in the first place. Then, encourage the new players to attend a training session before they decide to join – make sure you impress potential members with a fun experience that caters to their interests and needs. If you do this, it is more likely that they will return and eventually join your club.

The Coach

The coach will play a vital role in retaining and attracting new players. Therefore, each coach should be made aware of or given training on how to welcome new players, how to make their sessions fun and how to speak to kids at a certain age. In addition, coaches must communicate with the parents weekly via text, email or phone regarding team news.

THINK

Organise an open day. Approach your local school to get kids interested in attending a youth session at your club.

Used with permission from Shutterstock/PeopleImages.com - Yuri A.

How to Retain Players

To retain players, you need to be more than just a sports club.

Generally, players get involved:

- To have fun
- To make friends
- To learn new skills
- To build self-confidence
- To be part of a team
- To find an identity – to be part of a community

The sport/physical activity is often secondary to building the sense of self and community.

THINK!

Q What influences a player to stay at your club?

A The people, great coaching, great team culture!

Q Whose responsibility is the club and team culture?

A Everyone in the club, especially the coaches, players and members.

Tips to Improve Player Retention

While attracting new members and players is important, retaining your current members and players is equally important. The following outline suggests a number of areas to consider when trying to ensure you retain your current members and players:

1. **Provide a positive experience:** Your club must do everything to ensure it provides a great experience on a regular basis.
2. **Be a welcoming club:** The club must not become a 'closed group of friends only'; it must welcome new members. All club volunteers, coaches and players must buy into this philosophy. New members should be engaged from the start. Make them feel welcome and comfortable in the club.
3. **Introduce different formats of the game to suit all:** Some players or members may not be able to play competitively due to ability or age. Therefore, the club should organise a range of different formats of the game to keep them active and involved in the club community. This could include over-35 or veteran games, small-sided games or walking versions.
4. **Provide excellent coaching:** Coaching is one of the areas that can greatly affect player retention. It is important to ensure that you have recruited skilled coaches who are given regular training themselves. If the players admire your coaching, they are more likely to stay at the club. Not only will players improve, but they will also enjoy the interaction with the club and its coaches.
5. **Regular communication:** Nobody likes being left out. Therefore, it is important to communicate with members about the various activities in the club on a weekly or bi-weekly basis. This could be via email, WhatsApp messages or posts on social media.
6. **Get members involved:** Why not conduct an audit of your players, coaches, parents and members to identify their skill set? You may find that they have important attributes that can help the club to grow. Then simply ask them to get involved in projects throughout the year.
7. **Build team spirit:** Why not organise regular social events throughout the season?

Adult Men's and Women's Teams

The adult men's and women's teams at your club may be the focal point of your sports organisation. In addition, they are most likely your key income driver.

Having a strong adult men's and women's team takes a lot of effort and resources.

The following are key areas to consider:

1. **Pre-season training:** Creating a pre-season plan for the adult teams. Good pre-season training ought to include a variety of the following sessions:
   - Endurance exercises
   - Explosion exercises
   - Sprint exercises
   - Technical exercises
   - Tactical sessions

2. **Weekly training programme:** It is a good practice to have a training programme for your club in place. Each coach will have the flexibility to adopt their sessions but it should follow a similar format. For example:
   1. Warm up: 10–15 minutes
   2. Technique: 10–15 minutes
   3. Small-sided games (SSG): 15–20 minutes
   4. Game: 15–20 minutes
   5. Cool down: 5–10 minutes

   Obviously, the above can be adapted from sport to sport and may include a fitness session or other important activities, such as video analysis after training.

3. **Regular communication between the coach and the players:** This might include setting up a WhatsApp group and holding monthly/quarterly meetings.

4. **Regular communication between the coaches:** This might include setting up a coaches WhatsApp group and holding monthly/quarterly coaches meetings.

Final Thought

This chapter emphasized the importance of creating a welcoming club atmosphere and fostering a positive culture throughout your organization. We explored various strategies to enhance your club's inclusivity and make everyone feel valued. We also discussed the aspects of retaining current players while focusing on effective recruitment of new members. These elements are essential for building a vibrant and sustainable club community. The next step for your club is to meet, review this chapter and begin to strengthen your club as a welcoming place to attend. Now that you are a welcoming club, the next step is to ensure you offer great coaching at your club.

Used with permission from Shutterstock/Oleggg.

4 Coaching Culture
Getting the right coaching culture at your club

The most successful clubs focus on providing a positive and enjoyable playing and coaching experience. This section will aim to provide clubs with some thoughts on installing a great coaching experience in the club.

> In this chapter you will learn:
>
> 1. How to ensure you offer a positive coaching experience
> 2. Steps to effective coaching

Good coaching is essential for the development of players, success of the club, and fostering a positive experience. It goes beyond teaching skills; it shapes players into well-rounded individuals on and off the field. Clubs should provide frequent communication and training for coaches throughout the season.

> Priority areas to adopt in your club after reading this chapter:
>
> 1. Develop a coach training program
> 2. Organise regular training for coaches throughout the season

A positive coaching culture is about:

- ❖ Recruiting coaches with the right attitude and a focus on both player development and character
- ❖ Being well organised for weekly sessions
- ❖ Sharing learnings on best practice coaching techniques – continuous development

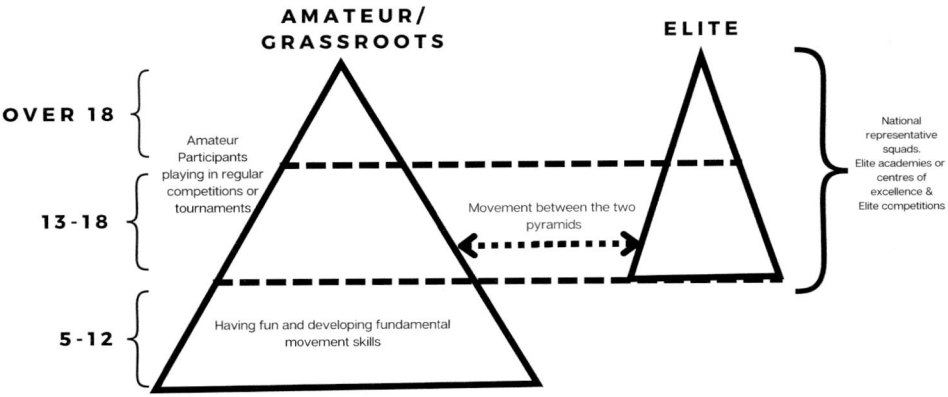

Figure 4.1 Grassroots and elite pyramids

The pyramids in Figure 4.1 represent the relationship and balance between grassroots and elite levels. A coach needs to understand this diagram in terms of the player and coaching pathway.

The first pyramid, representing amateur sports, has a wide foundation comprising grassroots participation, recreational players and community-level competitions. This base provides a large talent pool. As individuals progress, they move through age-appropriate levels of structured training and competition, gradually narrowing towards the top of the amateur structure, which includes highly competitive amateur athletes, coaches and referees. This pyramid emphasises accessibility and development, serving as the feeder system for elite-level sports.

The elite sports pyramid, by contrast, is narrower and focuses on the highest levels of athletic performance. This pyramid is sustained by the talent and resources emerging from the broader amateur base. It is common for athletes, coaches and referees to move back to the amateur or grassroots pyramid. It is vital for the youth and adults to be competing against other elite athletes on a regular basis. At its apex are senior elite athletes, coaches and referees competing at national, international and professional levels, supported by specialized programmes.

Together, the two pyramids form a symbiotic relationship: The amateur base drives the growth of talent and fosters sports culture, while the elite level promotes visibility and aspiration, feeding back into participation and interest across all levels of the sport. The age levels can differ from sport to sport (5–12, 13–18 and over 18s).

Offer a Positive Coaching Experience

Coach education is a key component of any governing body strategic plan.

Coaches at all levels play a crucial role in ensuring that playing sport is an enjoyable experience for everyone; coaching is also key in developing team's skills and creating better players. Creating a positive coaching experience, building trust with the parents and players and maintaining a player engagement throughout the season are vital elements to get right.

REMEMBER

Get the coaches together annually to refresh and discuss the coaching philosophy, ensuring they are all on board. Communicate the philosophy to all club members via usual channels.

Training Session Checklist

	✓	Notes
1. How many players are taking part in the session?	☐	
2. Have you written a session plan?	☐	
3. Have you written down the objectives of the session in your plan?	☐	
4. Do you have sufficient equipment (balls, bibs, cones, hurdles, goals) for the session?	☐	
5. Have you confirmed with the Academy Director if the facility has been booked?	☐	
6. Have you informed the players of the date and time of the session?	☐	

You can find a blank copy of the "Training Session Planner" in the appendix.

REMEMBER

Ensure the sizes of the training area correlate with the age of our team and length of each game.

Coaching Development

Coaches Personal Development Plan

Coaches must take ownership of their personal development. Key elements to consider include:

- Organising internal coaching sessions (Exchange learnings with your club's coaches.)
- Attending coaching seminars and webinars (organised by the governing body)
- Organising webinars or seminars with coaches from other clubs
- Attending personal development courses (Key areas include safeguarding, first aid, how to create a team, how to manage people, how to coach adults and youth players etc.)

Coach Development and Training

It is hoped that talented, enthusiastic coaches and a strong coaching programme will give the club a strong foundation to be successful. Each club should spend time identifying the right coaches to bring to the club, as well as providing regular training, education (at all levels) and knowledge-exchange workshops for all your coaches.

Coaches must hold appropriate qualifications and be committed to continuous professional development. It is not enough to acquire a qualification and then assume your training is complete. Training and education for coaches must be ongoing and continue each year.

Coaches must also receive clear guidance from the club (specifically the head coach or academy director) in terms of their roles and responsibilities. The Head Coach can do this through regular coaching meetings and workshops at the club.

The Academy Director should use the template shown in Figure 4.2 to record the current qualifications and training to be arranged for all the coaches in the club.

Coaches Name	Current qualifications	Date of expiry	Current team coaching in the club	Training to be arranged and the training provider	Date for training
George McCrory	Level 1 in Basketball	Apr 202x	U14 boys	Safeguarding training with the governing body	19 June 20xx
Joanne McCrory	No qualification	N/A	U14 girls	Grassroots coaching award with the governing body	20 June 20xx

Figure 4.2 Record of current coaches qualifications and training required

> You can find a blank copy of the "Coaches Qualification Record" template in the appendix.

Used with permission from Shutterstock/Drazen Zigic.

CONTINUOUS DEVELOPMENT

- Assign a coaching team to remain with a specific under-age team right through, from junior to U-19.
- Train your coaches by holding quarterly education sessions.

Coach Development Process

Key areas to consider include:

- Identify an academy or youth director at your club: Someone who has the right temperament, skill set and knowledge of coaching and understanding of the sport.
- Set up a workshop with the coaches to identify training and education requirements.
- Develop a coaching plan for your club. This will include an audit of existing coaching knowledge and skills, a plan to improve the knowledge and skills of coaches, an understanding of other club's coaching standards, resources required (attend courses, in-house training etc.) and costs.
- Identify the potential trainers and courses that can help improve the skills of coaches. Suitable trainers might be sourced from the national governing body, from another club, or simply they might be a member within your own club. These courses might be official online courses or coaching events organised by the governing body.

Coaches are critical to a players' impression of a club because the coach is often the individual who they interact with the most.

Coaches act as facilitators, motivators, empathisers and educators but they must 'buy into' the club culture and coaching ethos.

Also, don't forget that coach retention can be an issue, so working with your coaches to ensure that they are happy and motivated is an important consideration for a club.

> **THINK**
>
> What makes a good coach? An effective coach will be positive, enthusiastic, supportive, trusting, focused, goal-oriented, knowledgeable, observant, respectful, patient and a clear communicator.

> **THINK**
>
> What makes a great coaching club? A coaching philosophy that is understood and shared by all the coaches, and is then communicated to all members.

Seven Steps to Effective Coaching

1. Put players first.
2. Define coaching objectives. Be clear on your principles of play and ensure they come across in all your coaching sessions.
3. Understand the players' characters and skills. Develop each player's technical abilities. All players deserve the chance to get better no matter what their current skill level is.
4. Set realistic, and age-appropriate, development goals.
5. Offer a challenging and supportive environment.
6. Create a team spirit. Create a positive environment and build trust with each player.
7. Set clear team values, for example, teamwork, respect etc. Reinforce the values regularly throughout the season.

Final Thought

In this chapter, we highlighted the importance of establishing a strong coaching setup within your club. This involves recruiting skilled coaches and providing them with the necessary training and tools for success, such as session plans and resources. The next step for your club is to meet, review this chapter, and assess your current coaching setup. Following that, it's crucial to focus on attracting more female participants to enhance diversity and inclusion within your club.

Used with permission from Shutterstock/PeopleImages.com - Yuri A.

5 Female Participation
Increasing female participation at your club

This chapter outlines how female participation is developed in the club, from committee representation, to participation and coaching. It is important that the leadership and board members actively support and promote female participation throughout the club.

> In this chapter you will gain a greater understanding:
>
> 1. Why gender balance is important in decision-making
> 2. How to have female-friendly facilities
> 3. How to grow female participation

Healthy and Active

Participation in sport at any level, from grassroots to elite, contributes to healthy and active living. A club should want everyone to be equally able to experience the joy of playing in a team, or achieving a personal best, with the boost to physical and emotional well-being from staying active, and the associated benefits for their academic achievement, careers and family life.

> Priority areas to adopt in your club after reading this chapter:
>
> 1. Ensure you have female-friendly facilities at your club
> 2. Begin to attract more girls and women to your club

Female Committee Representation

Female representation on boards and committees is improving year on year. It is recommended that you have a diverse and balanced membership on your club's board and various committees. A good rule of thumb is to have a minimum of 40 per cent women and 40 per cent men; the remaining 20 per cent can be discretionary, depending on your organisation's skill set and diversity needs.

There is substantive evidence that greater gender balance increases the performance of boards and improves key decision-making.

Gender Balance in Decision-Making

Gender-balanced leadership benefits clubs through access to the entire pool of talent among the membership and parents, offering broader thinking and perspectives, and increased understanding of and responsiveness to members' requirements.

Improved gender diversity in a club can lead to positive changes in the behaviour of all members, as well as improving governance, culture and risk management. Balance among the genders on club committees generates greater ethical behaviour and improves decision-making.

There are many advantages to having gender-balanced board and committees:

- Enhanced dialogue
- Stronger decision-making, including understanding the value of dissent
- Higher quality monitoring of, and guidance to, management
- Positive changes to the club environment and culture

Increasing Female Representation

The club will benefit from more females on committees and in the club's management. Here are some ways to do this:

Practicalities
Are there logistical practicalities that are preventing women from getting involved (i.e. timing, duration, location of meetings)?

Recruitment, Training and Retention
Are there any recruitment blockers preventing women getting involved? Who is being recruited to the board/committees and how? Often people ask their friends, or those known to them, to get involved, which can unwittingly perpetuate a network of men/'old boys' continuing in committee roles.

Role Models and Mentoring
Are those women who do get involved as leaders and coaches being profiled in the club (newsletters/website) providing a positive example? Is there a possibility to mentor or buddy new female committee members in order to support them initially?

Constitution
Identify any rules in the club's constitution that might create obstacles to attracting and appointing women (i.e. the need to have been a member for a certain period before serving on the committee)?

Policies
Do you have a club diversity and equality policy? Are board terms limited to a set number of years? Setting limits for serving is crucial for turnaround. It is also important to let people know that a position is vacant, and invite women to apply.

Pathways
How can you make the pathway to board/committee membership more female-friendly? It is also important to prepare for the future and create a healthy and inclusive pipeline of female candidates moving forward.

Transparency
Is the club open and transparent when it comes to its targets, policies and practices around females in sport?

Culture
The club's culture is critical. Is the culture 'macho', or is it an open welcoming one, where diversity and new ways of thinking are embraced? Is the club culture expressed throughout the club?

Female-Friendly Facilities

With the recent growth in female sports, it is clear that there is a need to provide more female-friendly sporting facilities that enable, facilitate and retain the participation of women and girls. Some young people perceive sports clubs as places that are not meant for them. Providing an enjoyable and welcoming environment on the first visit is paramount to helping women and girls feel connected – this is vital to ensuring that new players return.

Equal access to facilities to support and enhance participation is critical for women's sports at all levels, from grassroots through to elite. Not only are the facilities vital but it is also essential that the policies and procedures within the club are focused on equal and fair access.

Having female-friendly sporting clubs sends an important message to all girls and women, demonstrating that they are welcome to partake in their chosen sport; it is therefore vital that their club's culture is one that will facilitate and support female participation. Talking to women about how you can make your club more female-friendly will help you identify areas for improvement in your facilities, activities and communications. It is important to recognise that all women are different – for example, you should consider those with a disability or who come from diverse communities, or older adults who want to participate in your sport.

The utilisation of these considerations in planning female-friendly facilities will demonstrate a commitment to female participation in sport:

- Female players have equal access to the facilities and equipment, so they are not allocated 'hand me downs' from the men's team or the less-sought-after time/venue slots for training/games.
- The gym equipment offered is suitable for use by females too, such as the availability of lighter weights.
- Changing rooms, if unisex, have lockable doors on cubicles or shower doors.
- Club facilities are always kept clean and hygienic.
- Sanitary disposal bins are placed in every toilet if unisex.
- Adequate lighting is provided in the car park so that female club members feel safe.
- Operate a 'buddy' system to ensure that all female participants get to their cars safely at night, after training and social functions.
- Invite women and girls to provide input into how to improve facilities, moving forward.

The Benefits of Being a Female-Friendly Club

☑ Helps to attract new members, supporters and volunteers

☑ Helps to attract more players

☑ Diversification, leading to better decision-making

☑ Wider sponsorship and fundraising appeal

Used with permission from Shutterstock/Tatiana Gordievskaia.

Female Participation 113

A checklist for starting a women's team is shown in Figure 5.1.

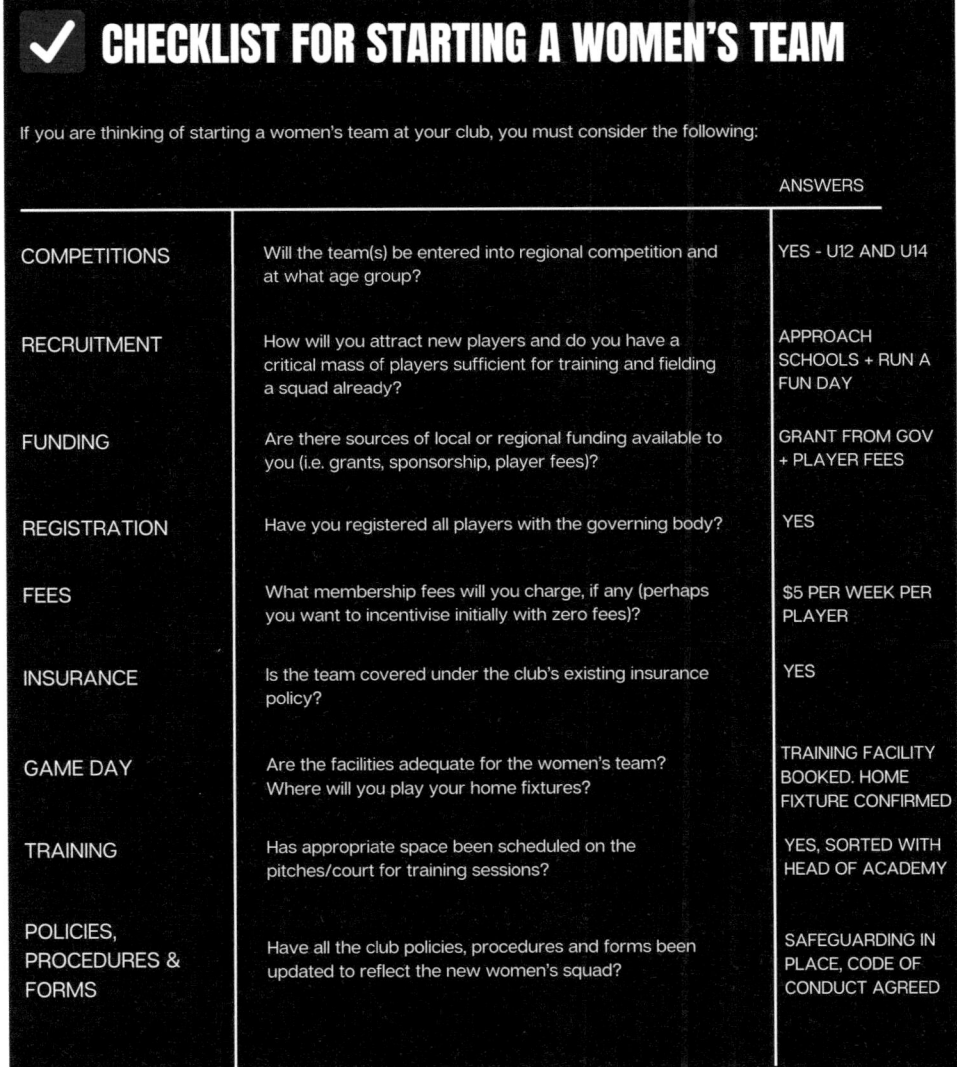

Figure 5.1 Checklist for starting a women's team

You can find a blank copy of the "Checklist for Starting a Women's Team" template in the appendix.

Attracting More Females to the Club

Attracting More Female Players

Throughout this handbook, we encourage you to reflect on your own club's objectives and strategies, or initiatives that will help you achieve these objectives.

Top tips for attracting more female players to your club:

- Encourage girls to bring their friends (word-of mouth is a powerful tool).
- Host free 'come and try', female-only days for players of all ages and ability levels, with no pressure on ability or results.
- Promote all your club offerings for female participation through as many avenues as possible, for example, partnerships with schools, etc.
- Existing players to bring their friends/family (and offer potential discounts for 'referrals' or family discounts).
- Promote to mothers the benefits of physical activity and playing sport.
- Ensure that your club is attractive to mothers by promoting the social side and involvement that exists for parents as well.
- Host a 'mothers in sport' day – mums and daughters can play/be involved in sport together.
- Ensure that fathers are involved when new young female players start, such as a 'father– daughter sport' day.
- Offer a holistic range of options outside of sport for new families, such as social evenings, trips to games or anything else that may help families feel welcome at your club.
- Offer a flexible variety of options at different stages of the season to ensure that people who miss registration/can't commit for the traditional season can still participate in sport.

Female Sport Week

Organising a female sport week is a great way to shine the spotlight on girls and women in sport and grow female participation at the grassroots level.

As part of female sport week, clubs facilitate an event/activity which could include:

- Skills session
- Club BBQ
- 'Come and try' club training session
- Club interviews
- Female support person day
- Game-day mascot

Used with permission from Shutterstock/JoeSAPhotos.

Female Coaching

Good communication with girls is critical, and the social aspect cannot be ignored. Being allowed to play with your friends, feeling welcomed and part of the club and supported by good coaches will help player retention.

When coaching females, regardless of whether the coach is male or female, trust, respect and effective communication are the keys to a positive experience for all involved. This will happen when the coach's behaviour is:

- ❖ Consistent, regardless of the situation
- ❖ Mature, showing that the coach respects the player
- ❖ Transparent, with a clear decision-making process

Tips for Recruiting Female Coaches

- ❖ Use current and former players who are enthusiastic and have the time to commit.
- ❖ Offer value add-ons for players who coach – discounted playing fees, compensation for their time.
- ❖ Reward existing coaches in tangible and visible ways – create interest and excitement around coaching at your club.

- Advertise locally: Social media (Facebook, Instagram etc.), local community centres etc.
- Pair new coaches up with a friend in a similar situation and have them coach 'as a team' to start with – this allows for flexibility of commitment and gives an instant, inbuilt support network.
- Target university students (students may be more flexible timewise and could be studying a related topic).
- Find ways that you can make an introduction to coaching less intimidating. Ensure that each new, and aspiring, coach has an experienced mentor who is enthusiastic, patient and welcoming. Introduce them gradually – use holiday camps or bring them to sessions sporadically throughout the season until they feel they are ready to commit for the season.
- Hold an introductory course for all current senior players, to gauge interest in coaching.

Final Thought

In this chapter, we delved into the importance of increasing female participation in your club. We discussed practical strategies to boost involvement, such as ensuring female-friendly facilities and providing tips for recruiting female coaches. The next step for your club is to meet, review this chapter and identify ways to create a more female-friendly environment to attract women to your club. In the next chapter, we will emphasise the importance of maintaining a clean club as a fundamental aspect of this effort.

Used with permission from Shutterstock/vectorfusionartic.

6 Protecting Your Club
Building a positive reputation for your club

Every sports club must ensure it has a good reputation, and positive behaviour and attitude are maintained throughout the organisation. In addition, every person involved in the club must be treated with respect and dignity, and is safe and protected from abuse.

This section aims to demonstrate the key areas for protecting your club, how clubs can tackle inappropriate behaviour and how to prevent it.

> In this chapter you will learn:
>
> 1. Tips to protect your club
> 2. How to approach key areas such as gambling and drugs

The key areas in protecting your club involve:

1. Smoking
2. Alcohol consumption
3. Anti-bulling
4. Anti-drugs
5. Anti-gambling
6. Anti-racism
7. Safeguarding

> Priority area to adopt in your club after reading this chapter:
>
> Develop a statement regarding the clubs stance on bullying, racism, smoking and drug abuse. Place the statement on your noticeboard and communicate to parents, coaches, players and members.

DOI: 10.4324/9781003650362-7

Welfare Policies

Club welfare means the general care and support of players, coaches, members and volunteers throughout a club.

No one involved in a sporting activity, whether they are a volunteer, player, spectator or elite athlete, should have to worry about abuse or harassment. Safeguarding in sport involves protecting children and adults from harm, by providing a safe space to play sports and be active. Everyone has a role to play in keeping others safe and people should know what steps to take if they have any concerns.

There are a range of club policies that are concerned with welfare, including those related to smoking, gambling, alcohol and drugs.

Smoking

Smoking should be banned in the spectator areas of all sports grounds during organised sporting events. Your local legislation will outline if smoking applies to all sports grounds whether council, public or privately owned and operated. An area to consider is to designate club premises as smoke-free, including e-cigarettes and vaping devices or simply identify a specific area for smokers within the facility.

The following policies should be applied to all sports-related events (including games and social functions):

a. No smoking shall occur at or near any sporting event or competition involving persons under 18, and this policy applies to all coaches, players, officials and volunteers.
b. Social functions shall be smoke free, with smoking only permitted in designated outdoor smoking areas.

Alcohol Consumption

Strict guidelines must be in place regarding the responsible consumption of alcohol.

Policies around the responsible service and consumption of alcohol should be practised at all clubs and should entail the following:

a. Ensure that light alcohol and soft drinks are always available as alternatives to full strength alcohol.
b. Wherever possible, food is available when alcohol is available.
c. Board/committee members should attend occasions where alcohol is served, to ensure that appropriate practices are followed.
d. A rule should be applied across the club that under no circumstances should a player or coach turn up to training or a game under the influence of alcohol.
e. Anyone under the legal age will not be served alcohol under any circumstance.

Suggested Process to Deal with Alcohol Abuse or Misuse

1. Meet as a board to discuss the matter and agree how it will be dealt. Select a minimum of two board members to deal with the issue.
2. Approach the individual to discuss the matter.
3. If this doesn't sort out the issue, consider suspending the individual from the club until the matter is resolved.
4. Refer the individual to relevant support organisations to help them overcome their issues or alcohol misuse.

Anti-bullying

Clubs should be committed to providing an environment that is free from bullying. Being bullied can have serious consequences for an individual's health and well-being, and bullying is regarded by the governing bodies as unacceptable in sport.

Bullying is characterised by repeated, unreasonable behaviour directed at a person or group of persons, creating a risk to health and safety. It can involve victimisation, humiliation, threats, degradation, offence and intimidation of another, potentially resulting in the victim suffering injury to health and mind.

The following types of behaviour, where repeated or as part of a pattern of behaviour, could be considered as bullying:

- Verbal abuse including shouting, swearing, teasing and making belittling remarks
- Unjustified criticism
- Excluding or isolating an individual
- Spreading malicious rumours
- Psychological harassment such as intimidation

Anti-drugs

Grassroots sports organisations must protect themselves from illegal drugs entering their club. The presence of illegal drugs can tarnish a club's image, leading to a loss of sponsors, members, and public trust. In grassroots and semi-professional sports, drug-related scandals can result in sanctions, fines, and even exclusion from competitions. By actively preventing illegal drug use, clubs demonstrate a commitment to fair play, fostering a culture of health and professionalism. This boosts the club's image and helps attracts players and sponsors.

Additionally, protecting athletes from drug use is critical for their physical and mental health. Drug abuse can lead to severe health consequences and can affect a player's performance at training and on game day. Clubs have a duty of care to provide a safe environment where athletes can perform at their best without resorting to harmful substances. By implementing strict anti-drug policies, clubs can support the long-term development of their player, member and coach, and ultimately contribute to keeping sports clean and enjoyable for all.

Recreational Drug Use

Drugs can alter a person's mental or physical state; they can affect the way the brain works, how people feel and behave and their understanding of their surroundings.

Young people can be particularly vulnerable to the effects of drugs, as the brain is not fully developed until a later age.

Drug use by members can affect any community or sporting club, and it is best to have had practical discussions regarding policy in your club before any incident arises. Including a section on drugs in your club's policy will ensure that members know what to do if there is suspected drug use or if someone is found distributing drugs at your club.

Practical Steps for the Club to Consider

To protect themselves from illegal drug use, sports clubs should consider the following:

- **DEVELOP A CLEAR POLICY WHICH IS COMMUNICATED TO EVERYONE IN THE CLUB**
- **ORGANISE ANNUAL 'DRUG' AWARENESS WORKSHOP**
- **CREATE A SUPPORT SYSTEM WHERE PLAYERS CAN GET ACCESS TO COUNSELLING SERVICES**

An Approach to Drug Abuse at Your Club

There may be a number of different reasons why a person will decide to use drugs for recreation. These include:

- ❖ Social pressures or to fit in
- ❖ Curiosity
- ❖ To feel excited and energetic or relaxed and calm
- ❖ To help cope with difficult situations
- ❖ As a response to trauma

Your drug policy should:

- ❖ Include clear behavioural guidelines for members
- ❖ Include clear instructions for what to do if there is an incident
- ❖ Provide responses that are fair and appropriate
- ❖ Position the club as a safe and responsible community leader

Dealing with an Incident
In the case of an incident involving illicit drug-taking at your club, take the following three steps shown in Figure 6.1.

STEP 1: IN AN EMERGENCY, DIAL YOUR LOCAL EMERGENCY NUMBER

Always focus first on the safety and welfare of those involved

STEP 2: INVESTIGATE AND RECORD

Once those involved are safe and everyone has taken a breath, a club official should record the incident in the club register

STEP 3: GET ADVICE, TAKE ACTION

Senior club officials should now move forward in a positive way, looking at lessons learned and preventative steps

Figure 6.1 Steps when dealing with an incident

Anti-gambling
Club members must never place bets on any game you or your team is involved in. This would trigger a conflict of interest that compromises the integrity of the sport.

If you bet on yourself or your opponent, you risk having your image and reputation tarnished, being banned from the sport (possibly for life) and potentially face criminal investigation and/or prosecution.

A gambling addiction (compulsive gambling) is the uncontrollable urge to keep gambling, despite the toll it takes on your life. A gambling addiction has the potential to ruin more than one life if unaddressed. Your club should be aware of issues around compulsive gambling and support any members who may be showing symptoms of gambling addiction to seek professional help.

Some suggestions:

❖ Organise a workshop on the subject of gambling and its risks. Identify the squads you want to be present and ensure that their coach/manager informs them and makes their attendance compulsory. Some research suggests that adolescents are two to three times more likely to gamble today (due to ease of access on smart phones, etc.) so consider engaging squads as young as U-16 up to adult

- Make sure that all club players/officials are aware of rules relating to gambling – especially the fact they are not allowed to bet on a game in which they are involved.
- Run through the content of the club's anti-gambling policy with members to ensure that everyone is aware of its aims.
- Run a gambling awareness night and use it to share the club's anti-gambling policy.

Check for Signs of Potential Gambling Addiction

Financial
a. Regularly short of money, even though they earn a wage
b. Borrowing money on a regular basis
c. Money going missing

Behavioural
a. Becoming withdrawn
b. Performance on the pitch/court is being affected
c. Seeming worried, agitated or upset for no apparent reason
d. Reporting feeling hopeless, depressed, frustrated or suicidal
e. Change in personality

Time-related
a. Being secretive about unexplained absences
b. Often being late for commitments
c. Taking a lot of sick days or time off

Anti-racism

Sports clubs must oppose all forms of harassment, discrimination and bullying. Racism takes many forms and can happen in many places. It includes prejudice, discrimination or hatred directed at someone because of their colour, ethnicity or national origin.

People often associate racism with acts of abuse or harassment. However, it doesn't need to involve violent or intimidating behaviour; take racial name-calling and jokes. Or consider situations when people may be excluded from groups or activities because of where they come from. Studies show that experiencing racism has profound effects on people's mental health and welfare. The effects can include feelings of sadness and anger, even anxiety and depression.

To dismiss claims of racism as just banter is to use sport as a shield for prejudice. It is deeply disturbing that this kind of racism may influence whether a player decides to take to the field of play or is forced out of the game for good.

The governing bodies are committed to providing an environment in which people are treated fairly and equitably, that is, as far as practicable, free from all forms of discrimination and harassment.

Forms of discrimination and harassment can include treating, or proposing to treat, someone less favourably because of a particular characteristic; imposing, or intending to impose, an unreasonable requirement, condition or practice which has an unequal or disproportionate effect on people with a particular characteristic; or any behaviour that is offensive, abusive, belittling, intimidating or threatening – whether this is face-to-face, indirectly or via communication technologies, such as mobile phone, computers and social media.

Some things you can do about racism in your club and community:

- Educate yourself on the issues of racism.
- Educate others in the club regarding the impact of racism. Develop a policy at your club.
- Introduce a procedure for reporting racism at your club.
- Support those affected by racism through working alongside a professional counselling service.

Safeguarding

We have already dealt with safeguarding in Chapter 1. It is vital for clubs to have a strong safeguarding program in place. This includes:

- Appointing a safeguarding officer
- Developing a safeguarding policy which is approved by the board and communicated within the club
- Conduct training on an annual basis for all your volunteers and staff (this includes board members, sub-committee members, administrators, coaches etc.)

Final Thought

In this chapter, we focused on the concept of protecting your club and the importance of maintaining a good reputation through positive behaviours and attitudes across the organisation. We emphasised that every individual involved in the club should be treated with respect and dignity, ensuring a safe environment free from abuse. This section outlined key areas to address in order to uphold a clean club ethos, including policies against gambling, bullying, smoking, racism, and drug use, as well as promoting alcohol awareness. By tackling inappropriate behaviour and implementing preventive measures, clubs can foster a healthier and more inclusive atmosphere for everyone. The club should meet to develop key polices and conduct awareness training in each area identified. Now you have focused on being a clean club, the next step is to fully engage with the local community.

7 Community Engagement
Becoming more focused on the community

A club is often considered a prominent organisation within its community. Clubs can embrace an entire geographic region with the services they provide and can have a positive impact on the local community.

This section aims to provide the tools to help the club become more 'community focused'.

> This chapter focuses on the following areas:
>
> 1. How to be a community club
> 2. Who to build relationships with in your local community
> 3. How to conduct a community audit
> 4. Creating a community engagement plan
> 5. Strengthening the community focus within your club

How to Be a Community Club

This initiative starts with the core mission of your club.

What is the purpose of your club? Is the club integrated into your local community, or is it solely about winning the league each year? (There is nothing wrong with wanting to win the league; the issue is that only focusing on results is not a successful long-term strategy if you want to develop and grow your club.)

> Priority areas to adopt in your club after reading this chapter:
>
> 1. Conduct a community audit
> 2. Develop a community engagement plan
> 3. Develop relationships with other community organisations in your local area

DOI: 10.4324/9781003650362-8

Making Your Club More Community-Focused

The following practices can help your club become more community-focused:

1. Ensure a community ethos is central to your club's mission, vision and values.
2. Recruit a community development officer (volunteer or paid appointment) whose role is to build relations with local community organisations.
3. Conduct research in the local community regarding the key issues and challenges being faced and what opportunities are available.
4. Conduct an audit of the community organisations in your area: Who are they; what do they do; what are they trying to achieve in the local community; who do they attract/target; does this organisation have the same approach to community engagement as your club; who is the key point of contact; what can we do for them and what can they do for us?
5. Develop a community engagement plan. Activate the plan and ensure that you have volunteers available to help.
6. Approach key organisations: Set up a meeting and discuss potential partnerships. Keep these partnerships small and simple to start with (promoting each other's events on your social media channels etc.), then build on that over time, to include long-term plans.
7. Keep the communication open with regular meetings with the various community organisations: Having positive and regular communication in place is important.
8. Identify potential projects that you can undertake together for the benefit of the community, and identify potential public sector funding for these plans.
9. Communicate with members every month via social media channels, website and email contacts, giving information about what the club is doing in the community.

Appointing a lead contact for your community programme is also very important. Clubs should appoint a community development officer to engage in a structured way with community groups, schools and youth organisations throughout your catchment area.

In addition, this individual should be responsible for developing partnerships with other sports clubs to ensure that your commitment to being an open, welcoming community club can be acknowledged locally.

Benefits of Being a Community-Focused Club

Being a community club has many benefits:

- ❖ You are able to help your local community by providing a great place to be active.
- ❖ You are able to provide a place where fellow teammates can meet each week. This in turn builds relationships and strengthens a sense of belonging.

- You are able to grow your club, in terms of players and volunteers.
- You are able to work with local businesses that are engrained in your local community.
- You are able to help the local community to positively tackle social issues through sport.

Sport and physical activity can help build stronger communities, by bringing people together.

By gradually engaging with groups and institutions from your local community, i.e. from women's institutes to schools or scouts, you will also connect with new people who will bring new ideas, members and skills to your club.

Community engagement works best when it's an ongoing process over a sustained period of time. The focus should be on building relationships and trust that strengthen community cohesion.

> **REMEMBER**
>
> Don't just think of other sports: Consider pensioners' groups, dance classes or other groups whose philosophy matches your club's.

Why Is It Important?

Your club does not exist on an island. It will be situated within a community of people, either rural or urban.

Your club should be at the very heart of your town, village or urban community. This will not happen overnight or at the 'flick of a switch', but through improved publicity, connection with local businesses, running of events etc. The most significant method of making this happen will be by involving the community-focused people in your club.

You draw your players (adult and junior), coaches, members, volunteers and commercial partners from within the community.

Not only will the community provide to your organisation but, in a similar vein, your club will provide for that community too, giving a place for people to meet, be active and maintain a community spirit that they can support and practice.

You want players who come into your club to feel a sense of belonging, not just to the club, but the local community.

> **THINK!**
>
> It is important to conduct research to:
>
> - Identify the need or issue in your community.
> - Identify local community partners to work alongside.
> - Create a community plan.
> - Confirm the source of funding for the project.
> - Ensure delivery of the plan.

Becoming a Community Club – Checklist

As a club, ask yourself the following questions outlined below:

- What are the outcomes/objectives we want for the club?
- Have you created a community engagement plan?
- Are the actions to be undertaken clear?
- Have responsibilities been allocated?
- Do you have the resources and experience needed within the club?
- Is the plan likely to be successful?
- Should you proceed?
- Is there a community development officer in place?

Building Relationships within Your Local Community

It is absolutely vital to create a strong and lasting relationship with your surrounding community.

A greater understanding of your local community will help you identify potential new members, players, volunteers and organisations with which your club could get involved. Local community relationships are critical for attracting players through initiatives such as club–school links or connections with other local activities or groups.

Having a local community presence helps support the wider, strategic direction of your club and, consequently, can help to develop and grow.

Having a local presence is critical when it comes to attracting sponsorship, as most local sponsors will want to know what local visibility you have. How many people on your membership database can they speak to (in line with data protection regulations!), and how often are you to be seen in local media?

It is important to be visible within your local community, taking up leadership roles in other organisations outside of sport that contribute positively to the health and well-being of the community.

Together with a deeper understanding of the issues affecting your area, your club can help to potentially tackle those issues through a community-led partnership programme, funded by a specific government grant or private foundation.

Community Relationships

The following provides the key stakeholders to engage with and build strong links in your local community:

- Other sports clubs
- Local businesses
- Local public/citizens
- Local council and politicians
- Local schools: Pre-school, primary and post-primary schools
- Local community organisations, such as scouts, churches, youth clubs etc.

Community Engagement Checklist

1. **What objectives are you wanting to achieve?**
   - What are the objectives? Are they achievable? Are the outcomes clearly defined with clear targets and milestones? How will you measure success?

Answers

Objectives:
1. We want to partner with a community group who has expertise in working with disadvantaged youth in our local area. The overall purpose is to attract 20 new players on a weekly basis to our youth teams.
2. We want to partner with our local secondary school. The overall objective is to organise two holiday sports camps during the year. This will generate £1,000 for the club in participation fees. In addition, we want to attract 20 students to our youth teams.

How will we measure success?
- Success will be measured by the growth in junior membership at the club.
- We want to increase junior membership by 20% within the next 12 months.

2. **Why are you doing this?**
   - What is the purpose of the activity?

Answers
- We want to grow the number of junior members at our club.
- We want to attract new youth/junior players to the club.
- We want to attract the parents of the new junior members to the club.
- We want more volunteers in the club.

3. **Who will be involved?**
    - Who needs to be involved and why? Schools, community groups, charities etc. Explain what is expected.

Answers
Who needs to be involved?
- A local community group that works with disadvantaged kids
- A local secondary school

What is expected?
- Community group – marketing to the youth regarding the club. Potential access to grants or funding streams (working with disadvantaged kids)
- School – marketing to the students regarding the details and dates of the football camps

4. **What level of relationship will be needed?**
    - Is it a light-touch relationship? (Don't pre-suppose the level of engagement that potential partners might want.)

Answers
What is the level of relationship?
- Community group – healthy involvement (six to eight meetings per year with the community group, weekly training session with the kids based on a defined programme)
- School – light touch (three to four meetings per year, organisation and promotion of two camps per year)

5. **What is the required timescale to deliver the agreed outcomes?**
    - What are the time constraints? Is the timetable realistic for all partners?

Answers
What are the time constraints?
- Community group – none. We can start this programme once the community group and funding has been secured.
- School – only time constraint is to have the camps organised by the start of the school term.

6. **What are the available resources?**
    - What are the resources required from the club to achieve the outcomes?

Answers
What resources required from the club?

❖ Community group – our club will have one contact person between the organisations. In addition, we will require the assistance of our coaching team. Finally, we will need expertise in completing a funding application for this programme alongside the community group.

❖ School – our club will have one contact person between the organisations. We will require the assistance of our coaching team during the holiday camps as well as booking a facility.

7. **How will you know that the objectives have been achieved?**
   ◆ Has something improved?

Answers
How do we know if the objectives have been achieved?

❖ Community group – number of new junior members recruited, PR achieved in the local media, potential grant secured (which covers coaching costs, hire of facility, equipment costs etc.)

❖ School – number of new junior members, £1,000 generated on the back of the two football camps

> You can find a blank copy of the "Community Engagement Checklist" template in the appendix.

Developing a Relationship with Other Sports Clubs in Your Community

Creating a relationship with other sports clubs can potentially allow you to reach a larger pool of potential members and spectators; for example, partnering with a local basketball club or a sports team that plays the opposite season to you.

Key areas to consider include:

❖ Opportunity to share facilities
❖ Opportunity to exchange coaching resources
❖ Supporting club events, such as fundraisers, for one another
❖ Potential to grow the number of members and/or players

Developing a Relationship with Local Government

Creating a relationship with local government will help develop relevant projects in your local community and secure potential grants.

Key areas to consider include:

❖ Get to know their 'programme for government'.
❖ Understand the programme for developing local government facilities.
❖ Get to know the politicians and their priorities for the local community and the possible role that your club can play in achieving these priorities.
❖ Know the various grants available that the club can apply for.

Developing a Relationship with a Local Charity

Spectators respond positively to news of their club supporting a local charity, as this benefits their community and shows what the club stands for, demonstrating the club's values and ethos.

Clubs should regard potential charity associations in the same way as contemplating a partnership with another community organisation, such as another sports club.

Key areas to consider include:

❖ Ensure that the values of the chosen charity matches those of the club.
❖ Ensure that the club creates an annual events calendar of fundraising activities throughout the season.
❖ Ensure that the charity partnership and events are well advertised in the local media and via the club's own marketing channels, such as social media, website etc.

Used with permission from Shutterstock/Ground Picture.

> **REMEMBER**
>
> The power of a sports team in a community is almost indescribable.

Developing a Relationship with a Local Community Organisation (Such as the Scouts)

Your community is made up of numerous community organisations that contribute to the local society. These organisations play a vital role in building community spirit. A relationship with a local community organisation presents the opportunity to run events that neither your club nor the other groups could facilitate independently. It gives increased resources and workforce – stronger together.

The strength of the relationship between your club and another community group is key to its effectiveness, so ensure that you maintain open and positive communications with any suitable group that you engage with and actively support one another's initiatives.

Clubs should conduct research into the various organisations in your local community to ensure that you engage with one that is a suitable partner.

Key areas to consider include:

❖ Identify the objectives of the community organisation. Do they match your club's?
❖ Identify which organisations are active in the local community and have a suitable reputation and brand image. Identify the target audience in each community organisation and the resources at their disposal.

How Do You Identify the Needs of the Community?

The needs that exist within the community can be identified by conducting the following:

Surveys

These can be either an online or paper survey. The recipients are asked to complete several pre-defined questions. It is important to ensure that you get as many people as possible to complete the survey and that the views of a robust cross-section of the community are represented. Refer to pull-out box for examples.

Focus Groups

These can bring together a group of local community members who understand key issues. The focus group will allow you to dig deeper into the detail. Refer to the 'Focus group example questions' for questions to ask.

Desk Research
This can be existing research that you locate online. Likely sources will be local government reports on sport, health, mental health, community cohesion etc.

Local Government Community and Strategic Plan
This document sets out the key priorities for local government during a set time period. It provides an overview of the key priorities of local government and helps you see where your club might provide support and assistance.

Focus Group Example Questions

- What is the club's role within the community?
- What are the key issues affecting the community?
- What organisations are currently working on solving these issues?
- What is the role of each organisation?
- Are they viewed locally as good organisations?
- Which organisation would you advise the club's board to approach about working alongside?
- Who is the key contact person there?

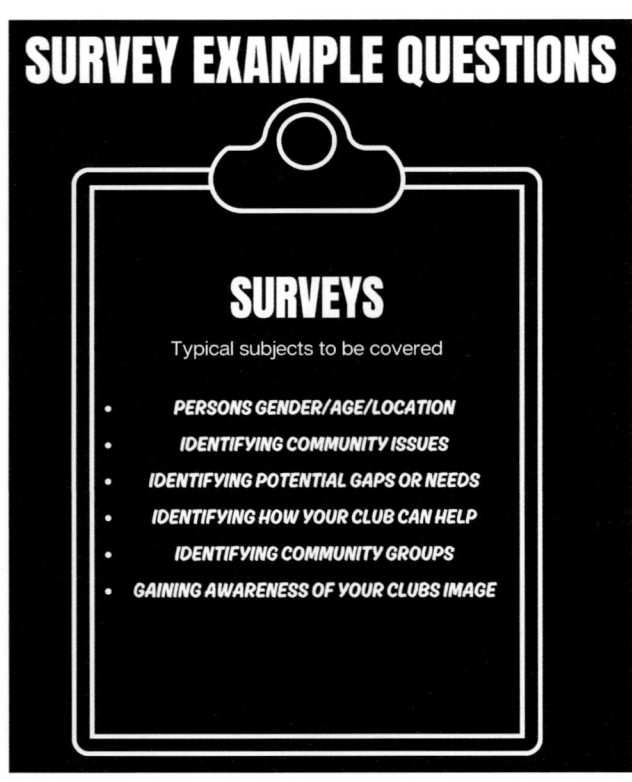

Conducting a Community Audit

It is recommended that the community audit is carried out within a three to five kilometres radius of the club grounds. However, the area for completing the community audit will depend on the dispersion of households in the club's geographical location and the number of other sports clubs in your region.

Key stages required to be undertaken by your club to complete an effective community audit are:

1. Define the locality or area to be covered by the audit. In addition, it is important to have a large sample size to ensure the results are robust.
2. Secure and train club volunteers who will run the focus groups and ensure the required surveys have been completed.
3. Conduct Research. Survey's should be sent to your stakeholders. In addition, a number of face-to-face focus groups should be organised to 'gain a deeper understanding'. Finally review key reports, data & government community plans to understand the issues in the region.
4. Analyse the information from the community audit (data, reports, focus group and survey findings).
5. Produce a report and send feedback to the board and your community partners.
6. Create a community plan and Identify potential projects that solve issues identified by the audit (either as a club or as part of a wider community collaboration).

The more people interviewed for the audit, the more credible the information obtained will be in the eyes of potential funders.

The main purpose of the community audit is to ascertain stakeholders' thoughts on:

- What key services are currently being provided in the area (leisure, fitness, community services)?
- Are there any gaps that might exist in service provision?
- What sports and leisure activities do you undertake on a regular basis?
- What is your level of engagement with the club at present?
- What additional events/activities could the club provide?

Once the research has been conducted (by surveys, focus groups and desk research), you are now ready to create your community engagement plan (see Figures 7.1 and 7.2).

COMMUNITY ENGAGEMENT PLANNING

STEP 1

Conduct an audit and research. Do an audit of what your club is currently doing with, and for, the community. How do you engage with stakeholder groups, such as schools and community groups? Conduct research in the form of questionnaires, focus groups and desk research in the community, in terms of opportunities and challenges / needs.

STEP 2

Set your objectives. What are you trying to achieve? Use the template (below) to identify your objectives.

STEP 3

Define your action plan. What are the tasks in your action plan and who will carry out the actions under each objective? What resources and equipment will they need?

STEP 4

What are the human and financial resources required?

STEP 5

Monitoring results. How do you plan to monitor the implementation of the plan? How often? What does a succesful implementation look like?

Figure 7.1 Steps to create a community engagement plan

COMMUNITY PLAN EXAMPLE

Objective	Owner	Timeline	KPI	Key Actions	RAG
Approach the local scout group to create a volleyball related programme	Chair	31 Dec 202x	One tournament held with the local scout group - 20 new players joining junior section	• Create one page plan for collaboration (e.g. tournament, coaching event) • Identify key scout groups • Approach scout leaders • Organise annual tournament • Organise four coaching events per year with the scout group	●

RAG - Red (unlikely to be met), Amber (slightly behind completion), Green (on track for completion)

Note: this community engagement template should form part of your wider club development plan.

Figure 7.2 Community plan template

> You can find a blank copy of the "Community Engagement Plan" template in the appendix

Strengthening the Community Focus within Your Club

It is recognised that most sports clubs are well connected to both their members and the wider community context within which they operate.

However, by adopting a more structured approach to community engagement and consultation, the club has an additional mechanism for people to become involved, feel connected and have a say in the club.

In addition, the information generated via community engagement processes will provide the club with a significant volume of 'needs-focused' data, which can support the development of funding applications.

Clubs can strengthen the community focus by:

- Including a community focus in your club's vision statement
- Including community-based values in your club development plan
- Demonstrating the benefits of working with other community groups by securing new grant funding, securing new volunteers, players or members
- Hosting joint events
- Appointing a community development officer in your club

REMEMBER

The best thing about sports is the sense of community and shared emotion it can create.

Community Engagement Checklist	✓	Notes
What are the outcomes/objectives we want for our club?	☐	
Have you created a community engagement plan? Are the actions to be undertaken clear? Have responsibilities been allocated?	☐	
Do you have the resources and experience needed within the club?	☐	
Is the plan likely to be successful? Should you proceed?	☐	
Is there a community development officer in place?	☐	

Final Thought

In this chapter, we explored the significance of community engagement and the advantages of positioning your club as a community-focused organization. We discussed the process of conducting a community audit and developing a community plan to strengthen ties with local residents and organizations. The next step for your club is to meet, review this chapter, and identify strategies to become more community-oriented. Looking ahead to the next chapter, we will dive into effective communication strategies and branding to further enhance your club's presence and connection with the community.

Used with permission from Shutterstock/Nomad_Soul.

8 Communication and Brand
Getting your communications and image right

Focusing on the club's image is not usually top priority for administrators but it is essential to get right.

> This chapter outlines the broad areas to consider as a community club, looking at the following:
>
> 1. Developing your club brand
> 2. Promoting your club to key stakeholders
> 3. Communications with the media
> 4. Event management

A communications committee should be established in your club. This committee will be made up of four to six people and chaired by one of the board directors. The purpose of this committee will be:

- To build a positive and consistent brand image in your local community
- To promote the various programmes and activities of your club in the local media and digital platforms
- To develop and distribute content on the club's marketing platforms, i.e. such as social media, website, email, messenger etc.

> Priority areas to adopt in your club after reading this chapter:
>
> 1. Develop an annual event calendar.
> 2. Assign resources to update your club website and social media platforms on a weekly basis.
> 3. Publish details of your games and events (use the same creative image, club colours, etc.) with the aim to increase attendance. This will in turn help to drive income.

Branding

It is important for clubs to think about their individual brand or identity. Your club needs to develop and focus on what makes your club unique. What is it about the game-day experience at your ground that makes it so special?

Branding is a complex area that some clubs either do not fully understand or don't have the skills or experience necessary to develop.

What Is Branding?

In its simplistic form, club branding is concerned with how people view and perceive your club.

Building a positive brand is extremely important.

Developing a positive and well-regarded brand for the club will help when:

- Parents decide which club to send their kids to
- Sponsors decide if they should invest in your club
- Spectators, players, members and the local community decide whether or not to be part of the club

Positive emotional affiliations and shared experiences with a club will create loyal spectators and members.

How to Develop Your Brand?

1. Create a workshop for key club members and stakeholders.
2. Create a list of words associated with your club's history, heritage and culture. These words must be relevant to your club. Establish a brand strapline: This is likely to be four or five words maximum and should sit alongside your logo in any communication.
3. Communicate your brand. The words you have selected must be used regularly and consistently to ensure that they are visible and acknowledged in all communications. So, if you are developing a press release, social media post or organising an event, you must communicate your key words on these platforms. A workshop should be held with players, coaches, volunteers and parents to ensure that they are aware of your brand and how you want them to play their part in rolling it out.

4. Evaluate: The club should conduct a regular evaluation of the communication and experience of various stakeholders to ensure the brand is coming across and being picked up. These will include a questionnaire asking questions, such as:
    - What is your impression of the club: Positive, negative, or neutral? State why.
    - When you see our logo, what words come to mind?
    - What can you do to improve our brand?

Your brand helps to shape what makes your club unique.

Key Components of a Brand

- **The club name:** Is the name of your club obvious to the location where the club is situated?
- **The logo:** Does the logo project a positive and modern image? Does it convey the club's history and heritage?
- **The pantone:** What are the club colours?
- **The 'tone of voice':** How does the club talk to its fans, players, coaches i.e. formal, friendly, playful, serious etc.
- **The typography:** It refers to the font style and arrangement of text.
- **Values:** What key values are linked to your club when people see the logo, or experience your club? Club members should display these key values so they are as visible to outsiders as the club's logo and colours.
- **Brand strapline:** The brand strapline is a simple statement which positions the club and succinctly tells others what it stands for. For example, the FC Barcelona strapline is 'more than a club'.

THINK!

Consider appointing a Public and Communications Officer (PCO) at your club. The PCO would deal with all things relating to publicity and communications, being responsible for the website, social media and media relationships. It would also be their responsibility to ensure the brand message is clear and consistent.

Developing Your Club's Brand

Figure 8.1 should be used as an aid for your club to clearly define your brand. Club members should sit down as a group to define their own brand words that are unique to your club (refer to the "Brand Words" in the appendix for a copy of the brand template).

Brand words	Explanation (what does the brand word mean to the club?)
Community	Our club will contribute to society, demonstrating social responsibility in our local community. The community will be at the heart of the club.

Figure 8.1 Club brand template

> You can find a blank copy of the "Brand Words" template in the appendix.

Process

Having discussed the branding with all members, the process mentioned in Figure 8.2 should be followed by the board when deciding on what branding the club will use.

1. Bring together the board and key individuals in your club for a workshop on defining your brand.

2. Before starting, clearly define to the group what a brand is and why this exercise is of value to the club

3. Write down the key components of the brand on A5 cards. Place the cards (outlined in this chapter) on the floor of the workshop room; if there are more than eight people, split the group into two. Each group should debate and select the most appropriate words. Aim to select 4-6 words.

4. Once each group has selected their words, they should come together to compare and discuss. They then need to select the key brand words as a group and consider why these have been selected: what to link to these words and the club's history and heritage.

5. After this meeting, brief the members, parents, spectators and various committees on the final brand words selected.

6. Roll out the brand words by posting them on the walls of the club and changing rooms, and posting on the club website, including them as often as possible in social media posts and including them in the club's membership rules, code of conduct and handbook.

Figure 8.2 Process for developing your clubs brand

BRAND WORDS TEMPLATE

- EQUALITY
- DIVERSITY
- EXCELLENCE
- PROFESSIONAL
- COMMUNITY-LED
- CARING
- POSITIVE
- INNOVATION
- RESPECT
- AMBITIOUS
- MODERN
- UNITY
- TEAMWORK
- PROGRESSIVE
- OTHER....

THINK

Don't be overwhelmed by all of the tasks and activities in this chapter. Resources and volunteers will both play a crucial role in delivering the various elements of this and all parts of the handbook.

If you don't have the volunteers to count on, don't worry: Just select the key elements relative to your club's current situation and implement those first.

Areas to Consider When Developing a Positive Brand Image

1. **Agree on the logo, colour palette and typography.** The logo is a symbol that represents the club and will be a part of the brand. Choose a colour palette and typography that are distinctive and used consistently across all marketing platforms
2. **Agree on the brand words and strapline.** Create a brand guidelines document which outlines how your brand is to be presented on the various marketing platforms (using the logo, the club's colours, font, use of straplines etc.).
3. **Develop a list of marketing platforms** aimed at your key stakeholders.
4. **Communicate your key messages and brand values on a regular basis** through your various marketing platforms. In addition, share the club's founding story, achievements and key milestones to build an emotional connection with the community.
5. **Be consistent in communicating your brand words** (use similar imagery, colours and wording on your website, social media platforms, posters etc.). Develop a brand voice that reflects the club's personality, whether friendly, inspiring or community-focused. Ensure all communication, from social media to email newsletters, maintains this voice and supports the club's core message.

Tips for Building and Developing Your Brand

- Create regular events at which the brand is promoted. These events should be used to generate PR in the local media as well as online.
- Consider linking your club brand words to a local cause or charity with similar values. This will strengthen your brand, as well as provide support for a great cause.
- Establish a connection with local media, providing them with a monthly column to cover details of games, as well as communicate key information from the club.
- Use digital platforms such as email and social media to promote the club on a regular basis, creating content regarding the club or players, members, parents, local politicians, etc. (ensure your brand words and strapline are used on these marketing platforms).
- Create your own hashtag, linked to your brand, and ensure that your club members and players use the hashtag.
- Provide training to the board, staff and volunteers in terms of your brand, their role and why it's important.

THINK!

Consider using the clubs merchandise to communicate your brand. Consider the kit design and launch of the kit.

Figure 8.3 shows a brand checklist.

BRAND CHECKLIST

Question	Answers
Have you created a brand guidelines document? • Consistent colours to be used • Consistent fonts to be used • How the club logo should be applied	Yes - brand guidelines document created Yes - club black and blue used on all material Yes - same fonts used throughout Yes - the club logo is applied consistently on your website, social media platforms and club posters
What are the brand words? What does the club stand for?	Community-led, welcoming, progressive
Do you have a clear brand tone of voice i.e. witty, playful, serious?	Yes - welcoming tone of voice used in all marketing material
Do you have a list of brand templates in place to ensure a consistent roll-out of your brand? • Powerpoint visuals • Club letterheaded document • Email newsletter	No - we do not have a club powerpoint background template but we do have a letterheaded document Yes - email newsletter exists in line with the clubs brand and colours
Does the content you post across digital platforms communicate your brand?	No - we need to use a more welcoming tone in our posts on social media
What actions need to be taken to improve your club brand (identify three clear actions with an owner and deadline)	1 - use more welcoming tone on social media 2 - develop a club powerpoint background to be used at all club meetings and any external stakeholder presentations 3 - make sure our club colours (black and blue) are consistently used on our Facebook, Instagram pages and on web and club emails

Figure 8.3 Brand checklist

You can find a blank copy of the "Brand Checklist" template in the appendix.

Promoting Your Club

A promotional strategy concerns how your club is going to be promoted.

Promoting home games or club events can help to improve attendance and in turn, increase revenue for the club.

A strong promotional campaign consists of the same overriding message and the same creative image, across a wide range of marketing platforms. These include but are not limited to:

- Email
- Social media (Facebook, YouTube, TikTok, Instagram)
- Website
- Flyers/posters/signage (indoors and outside)
- Game-day programmes
- Adverts in local media (online or traditional)

Why Should You Focus on Promoting Your Club?

A. Promotion can help to raise awareness of your club's home games or events (including fundraising events).
B. Promotion can help to increase game-day revenue as increased attendance can help improve sales of food and beverages.
C. By implementing a promotional brand with a theme approach and message, the general public and spectator base will be able to recognise materials associated with the club, no matter which platform is used.

Marketing Platforms

As mentioned, your club has a wide range of marketing platforms. These platforms can be used for promotional campaigns and regular communications with members, players, coaches, parents and the current spectator base (Figure 8.4).

These platforms include:

- Conversations or by word of mouth – players, coaches, parents etc.
- Email (member updates, club promotions, forthcoming events)
- Social media (Facebook page and groups, YouTube, TikTok, Instagram)
- Website (blogs, videos, podcasts, Search Engine Optimisation)
- Club app
- Printed club newsletter
- Messenger

PROMOTIONAL PLAN PROCESS

A. Conduct research. What do spectators or members want from you?
Where are your spectators / members drawn from and what are they reading or accessing?
(are they on Instagram, TikTok, or reading newspapers?)

B. Confirm the overiding message

C. Create a promotional plan which combines all the key marketing platforms, ensure you cover the following:

- What are you looking at achieve? What are your objectives? Is it to increase attendance at games or increase participation of younger people at the club?
- Who are you targeting and why? Members, players, government, sponsors, etc.?
- What is your USP (unique selling point) and what makes you different to other sports / clubs?
- What is your message which appeals to your target audience? What is in it for your target audience?
- Where and what marketing platforms will you use to target your audience?
- What tasks are required in order to ensure you achieve your objectives?
- How much budget is required to create and implement the promotion?
- What monitoring and evaluation of the plan is in place?

D. Work with an advertising agency (or use a free online design tool such as Canva) to create the chosen image aligned to the overall message

E. Implement the plan

F. Monitor and evaluate the promotional campaign. Produce regular reports and stats for the board.

Figure 8.4 Promotional plan process

Promotional Plan Ideas

❖ Hang a promotional poster on the community board at the local supermarket(s).
❖ Print flyers and distribute them during training to the players and parents.
❖ Work with sponsors to promote the club on their social media platforms and websites.
❖ Print flyers and distribute them to the local school(s), so they can be handed out to the pupils.

- Organise a family fun day at the club, with a range of skills challenges, and refreshments, on offer.
- Approach your local media to cover the game results each week.
- Develop an email database of all your players, members, sponsors and parents so you can send them monthly updates on the club (ideally in a club newsletter).
- Club events (barbeque, spectator or member evenings, open day, awards night, business breakfasts, quiz nights, birthday parties).
- Flyers/posters/signage/press ads (inside the club facility or in community buildings).
- Messaging (WhatsApp, Facebook messenger).
- Media coverage and PR.
- Marketing activity of your sponsors on their various marketing platforms.
- Branding on the club house or venue (posters, wraps around a building).
- Online influencers or ambassadors.
- Digital ads (Google/Facebook ads, Instagram ads etc.).
- Merchandise (club kit being worn by all youth and adult players in your local community).
- Local activities, e.g. with local shopping centres, schools, scout groups, etc.

Clubs must try to increase their reach and engagement on a regular basis (increase the email base, followers on social platforms, visitors to the website, etc.).

For many clubs, digital communication is the most effective and cheapest method of communication with members, coaches, players, parents and spectators.

The following sections will provide your club with useful information in the areas of:

- Content
- Email
- Social media
- Website
- Building a database

Clubs should establish a number of specific marketing platforms that are most relevant and useful to you.

Content

A content plan should be created and used by your communications committee to help it create and distribute club-related content each month. It is recommended that the communications committee agrees on the main content to be distributed during the up-and-coming year. This in turn should be approved by the club board.

Eight Ideas for Great Content

1. Weekly game information: Scores, fixtures, team line-ups, etc.
2. Player of the week profile: Adult and youth players
3. Major fundraising events: Working in conjunction with the income-generation committee
4. Club news
5. Directions to your pitch/venue/clubhouse
6. Video interviews with your manager and key players regarding the game and forthcoming fixtures
7. Background information on your club: History, contact details, practice times
8. Selling of merchandise, providing information on the range of products available, etc. (This is not only for the larger clubs but also those with a strong supporter base, or large youth section.)

IMPORTANT - Consider the possibility of outsourcing the online merchandising operation and fulfilment to a local sports business or retailer.

> **REMEMBER**
>
> The content plan should be developed a minimum of four weeks before the start of the calendar year.
>
> Focus on the key events organised during the year. Ensure you leave plenty of time to promote these major events in your content calendar (i.e. start a campaign six weeks before the actual date.
>
> Planning for the full year may not be feasible for all clubs. It may be better to plan on a quarterly or monthly basis.

Process to Follow When Developing a Content Plan

1. Communications committee to meet and brainstorm content ideas during the year. In addition, the committee should identify targets they are looking to achieve. This may include:
   a. Increase the number of followings on social channels
   b. Increase the number of visitors to the website
   c. Increase engagement of the content (likes, shares, comments etc.)
   d. Increase awareness with the club's activity
2. Insert the content ideas into the annual content planner and assign a content creator (Figure 8.5). The creator is responsible for content and distribution on the club's various digital platforms. Set specific targets for measurement of each piece of content.

Used with permission from Shutterstock/FamVeld.

ANNUAL CONTENT PLANNER EXAMPLE

	Lead Person Responsible	Web	WhatsApp	Email	Club App	Facebook	Instagram	X	YouTube	Other
Jan										
Feb	Sam	Promotion of home games								
Mar	Sam	Promotion of home games	Profile senior players			Live updates from the youth tournament				
Apr	Sam	Promotion of the game				Live game updates			Interview with senior players	
May	Sam	Interview with senior players	Promotion of fundraising event			Interview with senior players				
June	Sam		Promotion of club BBQ	Live updates from the BBQ	Promotion of club BBQ					
June	Sam	Promotion of home games						Interview with senior players		
Aug	Sam	Promotion of fundraising event								
Sept	Sam	Promotion of home games	Promotion of club BBQ							
Oct	Sam	Promotion of home games				Interview with senior players				
Nov	Sam	Promotion of fundraising event	Promotion of the youth tournament	Promotion of the youth tournament	Promotion of the youth tournament	Promotion of the youth tournament				
Dec	Sam	Opening of the new changing rooms		Opening of the new changing rooms	Opening of the new changing rooms	Opening of the new changing rooms		Opening of the new changing rooms	Opening of the new changing rooms	

Figure 8.5 Annual content planner

> You can find a blank copy of the "Annual Content Planner" template in the appendix.

Next Steps
- Gain approval of the content plan from the club board and playing staff.
- Produce and go live with the content.
- Measure the impact of the content in terms of likes, reposts, engagement rates etc.
- Record learnings and apply them to future content.

Email Marketing
Email marketing can be a very cost-effective and powerful way to reach your spectators, encourage them to buy merchandise and keep them informed of all the great things taking place in the club. Through effective email marketing, you can send messages tailored to the individual member, by segmenting your marketing list based on their preferences.

Key Elements That Contribute to a Successful Email Marketing Programme
There are several important elements that contribute to a successful email marketing programme. Remember, it is important to provide interesting and timely content in order to increase the number of those reading your email communications:

1. **Cleanse your email lists:** This includes removing or amending any emails that are undelivered as the email address has been incorrectly recorded. For example, john@browwwn.com – should be john@brown.com.
2. **Avoid spam words:** For example, free, cash, £££$$$$ and using capital letters.
3. **Use short, effective email titles in the subject lines:** The subject line will determine how many readers open the email. Ensure that your subject lines are about 50 characters or less.
4. **Email content:** Increase clicks by creating compelling content. Ensure that your emails are well-written and will be of interest to your members, spectators and players.
5. **Include an unsubscribe link:** Remember that you're legally required to allow recipients the opportunity to stop receiving your email marketing messages. You should have an 'unsubscribe' option on every edition you send out.
6. **Email header:** Include a header with your clubs' logo so that spectators can identify who the email is from as soon as they open it.

7. **Images and text:** You should use an attractive combination of images and text within your email.
8. **Mobile optimised:** With more spectators accessing email through their mobiles than desktops now, it is imperative that you optimise your emails for mobile devices.

Email Tips

- Ensure your club's membership and player registration database is up to date with the most current email addresses.
- Attract readers' attention by using pictures/images in the email.
- Use a professional software package like Mailchimp to provide templates for email design.
- Use a professional club management/membership app such as Teamer (https://teamer.net/) or TeamApp (https://teamapp.com) to keep contact details up to date.
- Group your contacts so you can target your communications appropriately:
  a. Parents
  b. Members
  c. Committee
  d. Volunteers/workforce
  e. New members
  f. Lapsed members
  g. Sponsors and local media

Social Media

Social media can help a club promote various activities from fundraising events, youth or junior team games and club news, to interactions with spectators/members. Planning ahead can help you make the most of this opportunity. Before using social media, you should think strategically about what you hope to achieve and if you have the resources to manage those goals effectively.

You should consider the following:

1. **Social media channels:** The club does not have to be on every platform; decide which are best suited to your spectators, members, coaches, players and parents. For example, LinkedIn may help you to reach your audience if you want to engage with businesses and potential sponsors.
2. **Content:** Think about what will interest, entertain or be useful to spectators. In general, video is becoming more popular and therefore as a rule of thumb, the club should aim to provide four to five video posts, three to four photographs/images and one text-based post out of ten.

Note: It is important to strike the right balance between posting too often and not posting enough. It is recommended to post once per day outside of game days and a maximum of seven to ten posts (including game updates) on game days.

3. **Resources:** Decide who will manage your social media channels, including creating content and reacting to comments. Ensure the team or individual has the right skills and enough time to do the job properly. Consider if training is needed.

There are ways that you can effectively manage your volunteers' use of social media so that you can reap the benefits. By creating a social media policy, your volunteers will be aware of the club's boundaries and expectations.

It also helps volunteers draw a line between their private lives and their involvement in the club.

Components of Social Media Policy
A social media policy should include:

- A definition and purpose of policy: Outline what the policy is about and who it applies to, including those using club-related social media and those who access it in a personal capacity.
- The roles and responsibilities: Who will oversee social media activity and take overall responsibility for the day-to-day administration of the different activities?
- Comments on the use of club-related social media: What are the limitations as to what can be discussed, commented on or promoted via social media, to avoid potential problems or reputational damage?
- Comments on the personal use of social media: Description of what is seen as acceptable personal use.
- General rules for using social media: Including examples of inappropriate content and terms of use.
- Information on monitoring: You must ensure that any monitoring of the use of social media is carried out in compliance with relevant legislation.
- References to other relevant policies: For example, disciplinary procedure or anti-bullying policy.
- Policy regarding sanctions: Where it is believed that a volunteer has failed to comply with the policy, they will face the club's disciplinary procedure.
- Ongoing review and update: Provide details of who will be responsible for reviewing the policy and when this will be done.
- Adherence to local laws and privacy guidelines.

Website

A professional-looking website will project a positive image and provide online visitors with key information about the club.

The following should be considered when thinking about your club website:

Design/website layout

- Start with clear navigation. Organize your pages into logically-named categories. Visitors will not want to guess where to go, i.e. HOMEPAGE—FIRST TEAM SQUAD—PLAYERS.
- Apply search engine optimisation (SEO) best practices regarding keywords, meta tags, link building etc.
- Ensure that the website is available on all devices and that it is a responsive site.
- Make site speed an absolute priority. Research has shown that speed influences everything from bounce rate over user satisfaction, to conversions and revenue.
- Ask visitors to your website to sign up to your club newsletter.
- Ensure that a good database or content management system (CMS) is in place.
- Install Google analytics. These can be used to track and report on your website traffic.
- Include an online payment system to take payments for membership/player registration, kit etc.
- Provide interesting content/articles on the website. Find out what the spectators want.
- Be conversational in your writing style. Write copy as though you're speaking directly to the visitor.
- Eliminate spelling and grammar mistakes.
- Avoid long paragraphs. Shorter paragraphs make the content easier to consume. As a general rule, a paragraph should be no longer than three to four lines.
- Make your home page a 'to-the-point' summary.
- Let images help tell your story. Real photographs work best, not stock images.
- Include videos and podcasts.
- Ensure that search engine optimisation (SEO) is followed on the website.

This checklist should help to improve your ranking on search engines such as Google.

> You can find a blank copy of the "Digital Inventory Checklist" in the appendix.

Website Assessment Checklist

Area	Response
How long does it take for your website to download? ❖ Desktop ❖ Mobile Hint: Check out Google speed test.	0.3 second
Is your website mobile phone friendly? Hint: Check out Google mobile friendly test site.	Yes
Are there any broken links on your website? Hint: Check out Screaming Frog site to test links.	No
Are you using keywords in your content on your website? Hint: Check out SEMRush for researching your keywords.	Yes, using the club name, sport and our village name.
Are links from partner sites to your website in place? Hint: Check out Moz.com to identify website linked to your website.	No. We will approach our sponsors and ask them to place a link from their site to our club site.
Is the 'contact us' form up to date? Who receives this form?	Yes. Secretary of the club.
Have you all the tags in place – title tags, meta tags, alt tags? Hint: Check out SEMRush site for information on title tags, meta tags and alt tags.	Yes
Are you posting content on your website on a regular basis (daily/weekly?)	Posts are three times per week.
Is the structure of the website simple?	Yes. We asked five parents to give us feedback on the site structure. All stated the site was easy to navigate.

You can find a blank copy of the "Website Assessment Checklist" template in the appendix.

> **TIPS**
> - Ensure that each marketing platform has the same identity, including the club colours and logo.
> - Create your own unique hashtag. This should be linked to the brand position of your club. The hashtag should be consistently used in all content produced.

Building a Database

A database is needed to record data of your spectators, members, and their key contact information. An up-to-date database is of great benefit for easy communication with your parents, players, members and sponsors.

The commercial benefits of implementing a database within your club include:

- Positioning your club as progressive and modern
- Supporting your sponsorship sales programme
- Increasing brand exposure and awareness through regular and consistent communications
- Improving brand reputation through the dissemination of good news stories

Key areas to consider include:

- Ensure you collect the most relevant and up-to-date data on your players, coaches, members, parents and sponsors. This will include the following details:
  - full name
  - full address including post code
  - role in the club, i.e. parent, player, sponsor, coach, member
  - date of birth
  - contact details – telephone
  - contact details – email address
- Ensure that you are recording the data in a suitable software package, i.e. MS Excel or MS Access. Databases ought to be password-protected, with a back-up copy made.
- Ensure that you comply with your local data protection laws and regulations.

Spectator and Member Engagement

Developing a meaningful, long-term, deep relationship with your spectators and members is fundamental for your club.

This is easier said than done though.

Many sports organisations focus on spectator and member engagement during game days. While this is vitally important, clubs must also engage with their members and spectators outside of game days (see Figure 8.6).

Remember: While all clubs strive for success on the field of play, engagement should not only be active on game days. It is critical to focus on spectator and member engagement all the time! That way, when the results are not always positive on the pitch/court, the club can confidently maintain its value in the community, continuing to promote its purpose and the key brand attributes represented by the club.

IMPROVING SPECTATOR AND MEMBER ENGAGEMENT

1. Set up a team to manage the spectator and member engagement project

2. Conduct research. The research will take the form of:

   a. Online surveys and focus groups with your spectator base and membership/players. This research should identify their issues, challenges and feedback both on game days and non-game days. It should cover the key areas of communications with the club, the game-day experience, the quality of food and entertainment. The research should identify the issues/challenges, as well as potential solutions and ideas to improve the overall experience.

   Note: Consider using Google Forms, Microsoft forms or Survey Monkey to conduct online surveys

   b. A club member should conduct an audit of the current experience. Areas to consider include:

   - Cleanliness of the venue (i.e. stands, toilets, club house, changing rooms, etc.)
   - Quality and range of food and beverages on offer
   - Transport links to and from the grounds
   - Pre and post-game information. Non-game-day content to keep spectators and players engaged

3. Visit other sports clubs and organisations to see how they are implementing spectator and membership/player registration engagement programmes.

4. Based on the findings from the research, create a spectator and membership/player engagement plan with clear goals, objectives and action plans. A volunteer(s) should be assigned to this role to ensure the roll out of the plan.

5. Implement the plan. During implementation, the actions should be closely monitored and amended if necessary.

6. Monitor and evaluate the plan (this could involve revenue growth, spectator surveys etc.)

Figure 8.6 Process for improving spectator and member engagement

Communication with the Media

Communication with the media is not just for the bigger clubs. Even the smallest clubs can use publicity opportunities to appeal to their local spectator base/members and promote themselves online to reach a wider base.

The first step to gaining media coverage for your club is to decide who your target audience is and what form of media you should use to reach them. Ask yourself who will be interested in your story and which publications or media will reach these people?

Your target media may include:

- Your local paid-for newspaper
- Local radio and television
- National newspapers
- Consumer and lifestyle magazines
- Bloggers, vloggers, influencers or those with an interest in your sport
- Online news and sports media
- National radio, online streaming sports sites and television

Tips for Writing a Press Release

- Keep your title concise and include your key words.
- Your lead paragraph needs to announce your most significant news.
- Your body copy should range from 300 to 800 words.
- You need to think like a reporter. Remember, they are looking for a story that will satisfy the editor and readers.
- Always write from a journalist's perspective. Never use 'I' or 'we' unless it's part of a quotation.
- Read good journalism to get a feel for the writing style.
- Shorter is better. If you can say it in two pages, great. If you can say it in one page, better.
- Communicate the five Ws (and the h) clearly: who, what, when, where, why – and how – should tell the reader everything they need to know.
- Include information about the club/federation. When a journalist picks up your press release for a story, they should logically have to mention the club in the news article.
- If possible, include a link in your quote to your website – for SEO purposes.

A press release template is shown in Figure 8.7.

PRESS RELEASE EXAMPLE

HEADLINE:
State the headline of your press release. It must be short and capture the attention

Crumlin United Football launch summer soccer festival

WHAT:
Name of event

Soccer Fun Festival

WHEN:
Date and times

12 July 20xx

WHERE:
Location: include address and brief parking information

Mill Road, Crumlin, Co Antrim
Car parking is free with 100 spaces available

WHO:
How many people / what age / if celebrities will be in attendance

500 kids (aged 6-12) with 200 parents
Former national team player will be present

STORY LINES:
List three or so story ideas here. Keep them brief and simple (use bullet points)

1. Former national team player gives his support to the summer camps and asks clubs to sign up early and register interest
2. This is the 10th anniversary of the festival
3. There will be entertainment, live music and food for all the families

CONTACT:
Include your name, position, telephone and mobile numbers plus your email address

George Brown (Head Coach)
Crumlin United FC
George@brown.com
0000 000 0000

Figure 8.7 Press release template

TIPS

Research the type of sports articles that particular journalists write. Identify those with an interest in your sport or club.

Build a relationship with local sports and news journalists before sending any articles and stories to them.

When you have sent a press release, follow up with a phone call to ensure it has been received, and check if the journalist needs anything further from you.

Crisis Management

From time to time, a club may be involved in a crisis.

The key focus is to be prepared and have a process in place should a crisis arise. A crisis can range from a fire in the club house to a child safety issue. It is vital that the club does not hide from a crisis but is seen to deal with the matter in a professional manner, showing not only how you intend to rectify the situation but also what measures you are putting in place to ensure it doesn't happen again in the future.

Crisis Management Checklist

The following provides a basic process/checklist which your club can follow in the event of a crisis:

1. Bring together the crisis team. This may consist of the Chair, selected board members, subject specific experts and legal expert (if appropriate).
2. Establish the facts – what has happened, where, when, why and who was involved.
3. Nominate and brief the spokesperson.
4. Prepare and issue a holding statement.
5. Communicate the facts through relevant media channels: Regrets (we are sorry this happened), reason (here's why it happened), remedy (here is what we are doing or have done since it happened).
6. Brief the digital volunteer regarding messaging and posts.
7. Monitor social media posts and log media enquiries.
8. Prepare a media conference/further formal statements (if necessary).
9. Consider other areas of the club which the crisis may affect (i.e. youth teams).
10. Update the staff, volunteers and media as the situation develops.

Tips to Consider

1. Use your own communication platforms to provide accurate updates on the situation (social media, website etc.)
2. Consider recording a video interview with your key spokesperson regarding the situation.
3. Try and respond to a crisis within a short timeframe.
4. Ensure you keep your club volunteers up to speed on developments through regular communication updates.

Used with permission from Shutterstock/matimix.

REMEMBER

When taking a photo for the club's use:

* Be careful with group photos, especially if a photographer from a local newspaper appears. Photos containing lots of kids may not be good for your sponsor if you cannot see the sponsor logos on the shirts.
* Don't forget to bring a digital camera or smartphone with you to any club events.
* It is important that you get to know the sports journalists and editors in your local areas so you can send photos to them directly.
* Include an extended caption with all photographs.

Event Management

Events come in many different forms. An event could be anything from a home game during the season, a pre-season tournament, a grassroots festival or a fundraising event. Being able to host an event is a complex and detailed activity.

The club should consider the following:

* Set up an events team (this could involve your income generation committee, if the event is a fundraising initiative).
* Define a budget, both income and expenditure.
* Create a clear events plan, which includes the objectives of the event, and roles and responsibilities of team members.

❖ Ensure you think of the spectators and members who attend the event: How can you improve the event experience? Consider parking at the venue's entrance, food and beverage sales, signage to entertainment or exiting the event.
❖ Have a contingency plan in place in case the weather is poor.

Event Budget

When budgeting for an event, the organisers should brainstorm and list the associated costs. It is important that all costs are identified – from marketing, to event management and hosting, food and beverage supplies, to insurance and administration expenses.

The key to budgeting is to ensure that you have included all costs (so there are no hidden surprises) and that the figures submitted are as accurate as possible. Once you have identified all the costs, the next stage is to work with the income generation committee to identify the potential revenue. Again, it is important not to overstate any income figure and to be as realistic as possible.

Event Budget Template

The template shown in Figure 8.8 should be used when developing a budget for one of the major events that you are organising during the year.

Emergency Situations at Events

In the event of an emergency, your club must be prepared to deal with the situation in a logical fashion. The following should be considered:

❖ Create an emergency plan which outlines clear roles and processes to follow (including evacuation procedures in place).
❖ Appoint a first-aid officer who can provide initial care until first responders arrive.
❖ Ensure stewards manage crowd movement.
❖ Provide an update via the club public relations officer (PRO).
❖ Record the emergency on an accident form - refer to the appendix for an "Accident Report Form" and "Emergency Details Form" template.

> You can find a blank copy of the "Accident Report Form" and "Emergency Details Form" in the appendix.

EVENT BUDGET EXAMPLE

	Jan	Feb	Mar	Apr	May	Jun	Jul	Aug	Sep	Oct	Nov	Dec
INCOME												
Sponsorship				500	500							
Ticketing			100	100	100	100						
Food & Beverage						1000						
Merchandising						500						
TOTAL			100	600	600	1600						
EXPENDITURE												
Rent				100	100	100	100					
Security Costs				50			5					
Promotional Costs				50	50	50	50					
TOTAL				200	150	150	155					
PROFIT / LOSS				-100	450	450	1445					

Figure 8.8 Event budget template

Ten Ways to Create a Great Event

1. Develop your event goals and objectives: What do you hope to achieve?
2. Organize your team and identify one key event manager or event chair: This team should meet regularly to ensure a successful event is always delivered.
3. Establish your budget: Venue hire, staffing, marketing, entertainment, food and drink, security, etc.
4. Set the date: Give yourself enough time to plan and book the venue.
5. Create an event management plan: This should give venue and site information, logistics, catering management (contracts, permits, insurance etc.), marketing campaign, major incident plan, traffic management, volunteer management and training, risk assessments, security, health and safety, emergency services etc.
6. Brand your event: Are your logo and key messages on display around the event venue?
7. Identify and establish partnerships and sponsors: Providing in kind or paid sponsorship.
8. Create a publicity plan: Inform the local media outlets of your event.

168 Leading a Grassroots Sports Club

9. Develop an event checklist: Prepare a checklist, taking you through the whole day from set up to clean up.
10. Measure success and feedback: Ensure that you ask visitors to fill in a feedback survey following your event, or that you ask for their feedback during a one-to-one interview, so the club can learn from visitors' experiences.

Event Calendar Example

The template shown in Figure 8.9 can be used when you are developing an annual calendar for all your events – from games to fundraising to community events. All events should be presented on one page. This event calendar should be uploaded onto your website and social media platforms.

Figure 8.9 Event calendar template

> You can find a blank copy of the "Event Calendar" template in the appendix.

A post-event evaluation example is shown in Figure 8.10.

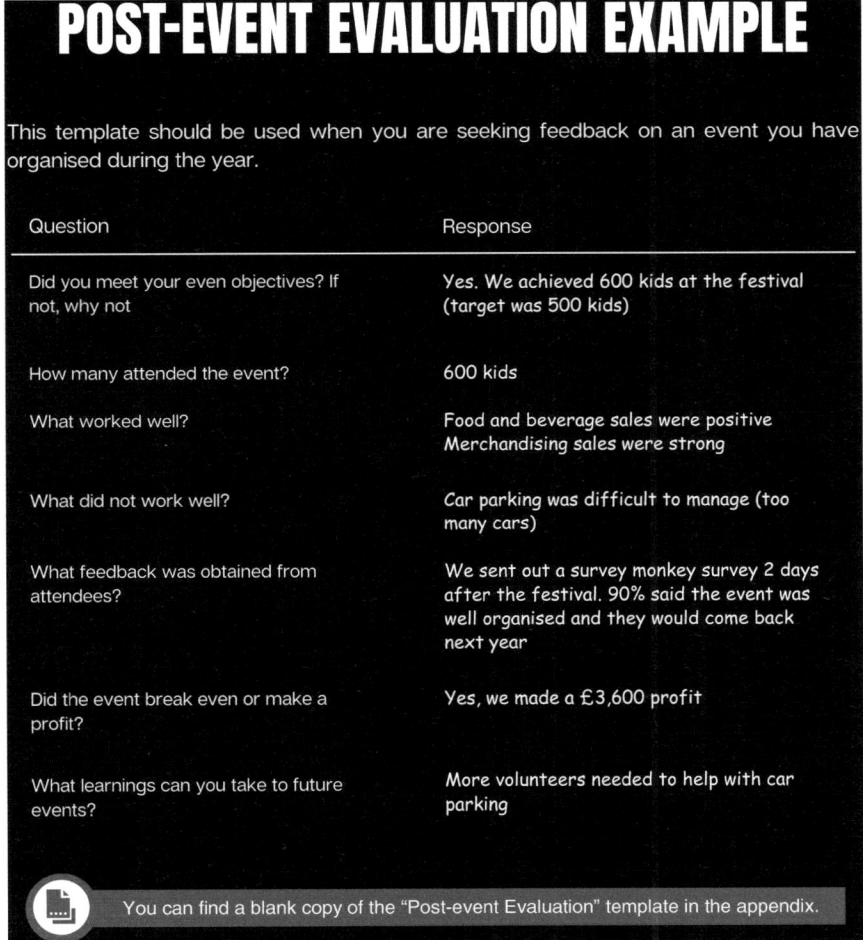

Figure 8.10 Post-event evaluation template

> **REMEMBER**
>
> No matter the size of your event, it is recommended that you create a customer service area where spectators and members can receive information about the event.
>
> The customer service agents must be given training on:
>
> ❖ Details of the event
> ❖ Location of key facilities such as the toilets
> ❖ Typical queries, such as the location of the first-aid room, location of the baggage room, public transportation and taxi information

Game-Day Planner

The following game-day planner should be used to assist your volunteers who have a role on game days. The purpose of the planner is to provide a list of the key activities to be completed by the club on the day. Having a game-day planner in place helps ensure that your game is well planned and executed, with nothing left to chance.

Figure 8.11 is based on a 2 pm kick off for a home game (football/soccer).

GAME OPPONENT		
DATE / START TIME		
LOCAL TIME	**ACTIVITY TO BE COMPLETED**	**PERSON RESPONSIBLE**
09:00	KIT MAN OPENS THE CLUB	KIT MAN
10:00	KIT HUNG UP IN CHANGING ROOMS FOR HOME GAMES CHECK THE LINES ON THE PITCH	KIT MAN
11:00	POST A MESSAGE ON SOCIAL MEDIA WITH GAME-DAY INFORMATION (K.O. TIME, OPPONENTS, INFORMATION REGARDING CANTEEN OPENING HOURS, ETC)	SOCIAL MEDIA OFFICER
12:00	MATCH BALLS CHECKED FOR CORRECT PRESSURE PUT OUT CORNER FLAGS AND SET UP NETS ON GOALS	KIT MAN
13:00	WELCOME THE REFEREE AND AWAY TEAM	CHAIR
	COMPLETE LINE-UP ONLINE POST LINE-UP ON SOCIAL MEDIA	SOCIAL MEDIA OFFICER
14:00	KICK OFF	
15:00	POST GAME UPDATES ON SOCIAL MEDIA	SOCIAL MEDIA OFFICER
16:00	POST GAME UPDATES ON SOCIAL MEDIA	SOCIAL MEDIA OFFICER
17:00	INFORM LEAGUE OF THE RESULT	SECRETARY
18:00	ENSURE THE CLUB IS CLEAN BEFORE EVERYONE LEAVES ENSURE THE CLUB IS LOCKED	FACILITIES OFFICER

A member of the board should meet with the respective individual to discuss their role and duties during match-day.

Figure 8.11 Game day planner template

> You can find a blank copy of the "Game-Day Planner" template in the appendix.

Final Thought

In the chapter, we focused on the essential elements of communication and branding for your club. We explored various aspects, including effective branding strategies, promoting your club, engaging with the media, and managing events. The next step for your club is to meet, review this chapter and establish a clear brand identity along with strategies for effective promotion. As we move forward, the next chapter will address income generation, providing insights into sustainable financial practices for your club.

Used with permission from Shutterstock/Anton Vierietin.

9 Income Generation
Bringing money into your club

Generating income is necessary for grassroots clubs to survive and grow.

This chapter outlines the key income streams available to your club and some useful tips and templates.

Due to the wide range and size of sports clubs, some sections of this chapter may not be as relevant to your club as others.

> This chapter focuses on the following areas:
>
> 1. Who should be responsible for generating the money in your club?
> 2. What are the various possible income streams?

> Priority areas to adopt in your club after reading this chapter:
>
> 1. Set up an income generation committee at your club.
> 2. Create a sponsorship sales presentation that can be used when approaching potential sponsors.
> 3. Create a list (possibly using Microsoft Excel) of suitable businesses to target.
> 4. Increase profit margins on food and beverages where possible (while ensuring quality).

Who Should Be Responsible for Generating the Money in Your Club?

Semi-professional clubs: It is recommended that these clubs have dedicated staff members solely focused on generating income each season. This dedicated resource should report to the chief executive (or general manager) and be supported by an income generation committee.

Community clubs: It is recommended that an income generation committee be set up within the club.

The Income Generation Committee

The role of this committee is to oversee the implementation of the income generation plan and to ensure that the annual income targets are met each year.

This committee should include club members with sales and marketing experience, as well as local businesspeople, who can provide independent advice and introductions to potential business contacts.

In community clubs, this committee will take a more operational role, where it will be responsible for generating the income set by the board. The committee will actively identify and meet potential sponsors, organise fundraising events, ensure membership/player registration has been paid etc.

This committee should meet once per month.

The committee should have a chair (usually a board member at the club), and several active club and non-club members who can share the workload.

Planning to Generate Income

An income generation plan should be developed. The income generation plan should include:

- Proposed sources of income for the up-and-coming year
- Targets for all income streams (such as sponsorship, food and beverage sales, donations, grants, membership fees etc.)
- A list of clear actions, with owners and deadlines, in order to achieve the targets
- A list of potential groups to approach, i.e. grant providers, sponsors etc.
- The monitoring and evaluation of the plan throughout the year; deciding how this will be done and by which date

The club can use an 'income generation calendar' to identify key revenue streams during the year.

> You can find a blank copy of the "Income Generation Calendar" template in the appendix.

Potential Income Streams

There are a wide range of income streams open to community clubs. Your clubs should review each income stream and identify which are most suited to your specific situation:

- Membership/player registration fees
- Bar/canteen revenue/food and beverages

- Fundraising
- Sponsorship (including value in kind)
- Grants and foundations
- Club facilities
- Donations/patronage
- Online digital revenue
- Holiday camps
- Ticketing
- Merchandise
- Other sources

REMEMBER

- The income generation committee need to identify what funds are required for the season ahead.
- Based on this information, the committee needs to ask the board how much profit (over and above the annual costs) the club wishes to make by the end of the year.
- As profits are generated annually, this allows the club to invest money in specific projects or, indeed save for a 'rainy day'.

Membership (Player Registration Fees)

The annual membership fee paid to the club can come in various forms, for example:

1. **Junior player registration:** Junior membership can be paid in one lump sum or smaller weekly/monthly fees and can include the cost of a kit and the weekly dues for a child's club membership.
2. **Adult player registration:** This is paid annually by adult players at the start of the season.
3. **Adult membership (non-player):** This is paid annually by adults who are not players but still want to be part of the club (maybe former players or simply supporters).
4. **Business membership:** This is paid annually by business organisations in return for benefits, such as branding on the club's website. In essence, this is a business club where events can be organised for networking purposes, and business can be conducted.
5. **Family membership:** This is paid annually to register a full family's membership of the club.

Figure 9.1 shows the membership process.

MEMBERSHIP PROCESS

1. The income generation committee should together identify the various membership levels at your club and assign one person each specific income stream.

2. Identify the annual / monthly fees for each membership level (this should be agreed at the AGM)

3. Identify the benefits / packages under each membership, i.e. discount on sponsors' products, discount on training kits etc

4. Gain approval of the various membership levels and their packages by the board

5. Agree dates to open and close the various membership levels (to be circulated by letter or email)

6. Develop various relevant forms of communication to promote the different membership levels

7. Monitor the uptake and then take necessary action if required, to drive membership numbers

Figure 9.1 Membership process

> **TIP**
>
> Set up direct debit payments for members and players. This will save time in terms of administration and chasing late fees.
>
> Offer monthly and annual membership payment options and reward those who make an annual payment with a discount.

Bar and Canteen Revenue: Food and Beverages

At each home game, clubs can increase income from spectators and club members who attend games. A main source of income can be the sale of food and beverages via the club bar or canteen.

This service can be provided from your facility's food van or a more advanced food and beverage kiosk area.

In addition to the bar or canteen, a regular barbeque (BBQ) at each game or family day is another potential source of income. BBQs offer a range of fundraising opportunities that can be considered:

- Can you host different BBQ weekends with specific themes? Maybe link the event to a film release or special dates, such as Easter or Christmas.
- Ensure that you set an attractive price point for the food to help drive sales.
- Ensure that the BBQ itself is positioned in a busy area during games to help attract customers.
- Purchase the food (meat, plant-based alternatives, bread, sauces) from local suppliers who have a good name in terms of quality. By buying local, you are supporting your business community that may then in turn help you.
- Consider the range of food on offer. Can you offer deals, involving purchasing food with a beverage or additional 'toppings', to increase potential profit?
- Consider leveraging value in kind donations of food and beverages from local suppliers, which can be sold on game days, i.e. burgers and breads from the local butcher and bakery.

In addition to the quality and price of the food and beverages, it is important to provide great service. The three important factors in providing a great service are as follows:

- Positive dialogue with your customers
- Developing ongoing relationships
- Having skilled staff/volunteers, with a positive attitude, who have undergone cooking and customer service training

Food and Beverages Tips

- The quality of food is key. High-quality food can result in increased sales but there will be potential cost implications of providing better food. Identify and work with local suppliers (e.g. why not approach a local butcher to see if they can provide some free samples that you can sell – then you'll be making 100% profit and the butcher will gain extra awareness of their products?).
- Ensure that you can offer a wide range of food, including some healthy options that are suitable for the spectator base and membership.

- Ensure that you have a sufficient number of volunteers on a rota system to staff the canteen/BBQ; ensure they are trained in customer service.
- If the volunteers are cooking the food, try to provide training from a local chef and the appropriate food hygiene training/course.
- Find ways to generate additional profit margins from the sale of food and beverages. A 5–10 per cent increase in prices can make a big difference over a full season.
- Outsource the sales of food and beverages or do it yourself; you will need to consider the commission rates offered by suppliers versus the potential profit margins to be gained if this service is provided by the club.

Fundraising

This a major stream of income for any club. However, it can take a long time to generate funds through fundraising. It is difficult to predict whether fundraising will be successful especially if the form of fundraising has not been tried before.

There are a wide range of creative and innovative ideas regarding fundraising. It is important that:

1. The income generation committee develops a list of fundraising ideas before the start of each season.
2. You develop a fundraising programme. This should be part of your income generation plan and will outline the various fundraising activities that are being organised, along with the details of when they will be taking place, who in the committee is the main contact responsible for each initiative and what the target is in terms of money to be raised.
3. You should focus on one or two major fundraising events during any given year, i.e. a concert or entertainment night, which can be supported by possibly two smaller events that would be easier to organise.
4. Your fundraising plans should not always target the same audience; it is important to broaden the scope of your fundraising initiatives to appeal to more people.

Some potential fundraising ideas to consider at your club are:

- A Q&A with a famous sports star (with entry charged for the event)
- Sponsored run or bike ride
- A musical concert or casino-style night
- Quiz night (charging for participation with prizes donated by club members or local businesses)
- A raffle (with prizes donated by club members or local businesses)
- 50:50 draw
- An online auction (there are online platforms available that will facilitate this)
- Produce an annual calendar (selling advertising slots to local businesses)

❖ Members offer their services (i.e. cleaning a house, washing cars) in an auction where the donation goes directly to the club
❖ A recycling initiative, collecting used mobile phones, clothes, ink cartridges etc. and selling them
❖ Offering bag-packing services at local supermarkets where members pack customers' shopping in return for a small donation
❖ A disco for junior members
❖ Loose change collection box in a local shop

Income Generation Process

Figure 9.2 shows an income generation process.

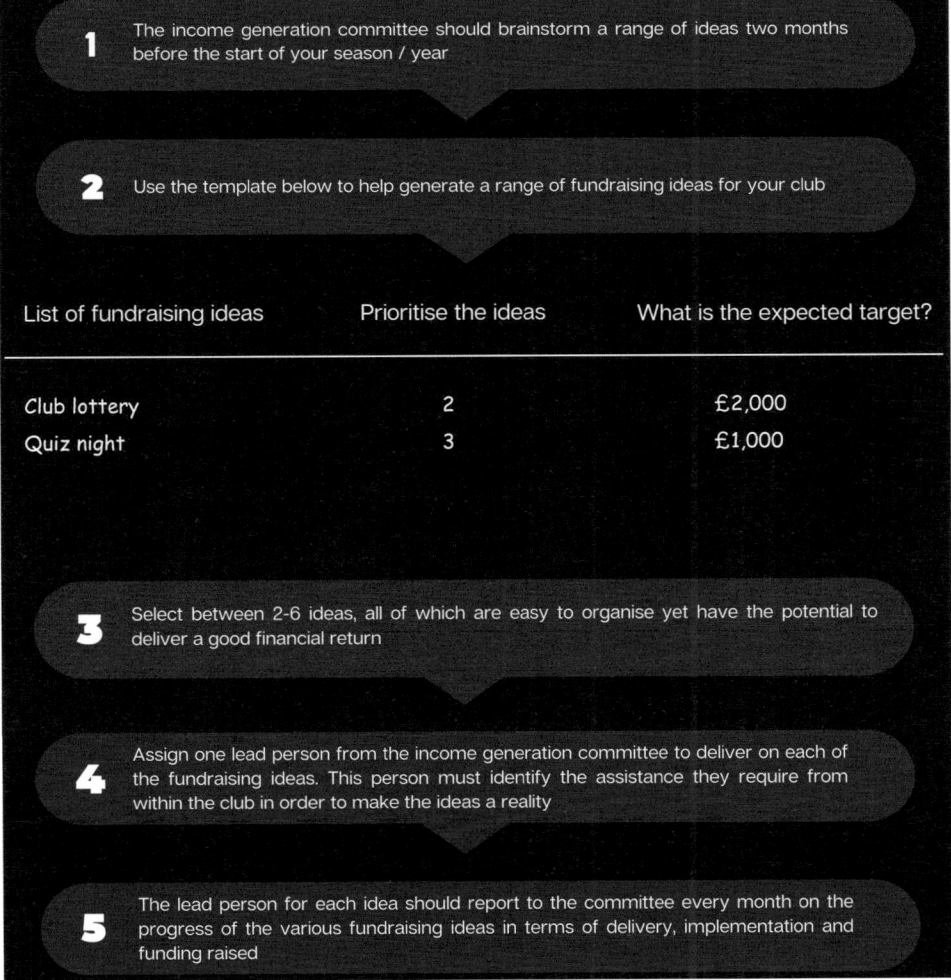

Figure 9.2 Income generation process

> **TIPS**
>
> Try not to focus on ideas that generate £1 per person; rather focus on those capable of generating between £5 and £10 per person.
>
> Ensure that you have a fundraising team in place to oversee these initiatives in order to spread the workload.
>
> Make sure you are aware of any laws regarding fundraising in your area before you start undertaking any plans.

Sponsorship

Sponsorship is probably one of the most obvious income streams, yet it is difficult to secure. Sponsorship isn't an ask for some quick cash, it's showing that you are willing to work with a business to ensure a long-term mutually beneficial relationship.

The income generation committee will play a key role in delivering sponsorship revenue. Some of its roles are discussed here.

1. **List all the assets for which sponsorship can be sold:** This can include placing sponsorship on the club jerseys, women's programme sponsor, the sponsoring of a youth festival or tournament etc.
2. **Create a sponsorship hierarchy and package for each sponsor:** A sponsorship hierarchy is a tiered structure that categorises sponsorship packages based on the levels of investment and benefits. It allows sponsors to choose from different tiers, such as platinum, gold or silver, each offering varying levels of exposure and engagement opportunities.

   Initially keep the package broad, until you have met the potential sponsor and understand their objectives. You can then present their specific package, listing all the rights and benefits they will acquire. See below some examples of what you can offer a sponsor:

   - Their logos printed on your kit or training wear
   - Product advertisements on venue boards
   - Their logo included on your website, email footers etc.
   - The holding of an event at your sponsor or partner's venue, or allow them to hold an event at your venue, i.e. a sponsored 'family fun day', held at your club house during the off season

   Note: Make sure that the club can deliver whatever assets/benefits are included in the sponsorship package to that sponsor.

3. **Assign a fee:** A grassroots sports club would typically assign fees to sponsorship packages based on the value and visibility they can offer to sponsors. Factors such as the club's reach (number of members, spectators, players and event attendees), the level of exposure (e.g. branding on kits, banners, social media mentions) will influence pricing. Additionally, grassroots clubs can create tiered packages (e.g., bronze, silver, gold) with varying levels of benefits, charging higher fees for more prominent placements or exclusive partnerships while ensuring the pricing remains accessible to local businesses.

    A grassroots club should consider the following approach when setting the fee for the package:
    - **Cost:** What are the real costs to implement the package? Each individual cost should be added up with a healthy profit added.
    - **Sales:** What are the expected sales to be generated on the back of the sponsorship? The commission level should be added up to identify the value to the club and sponsor.
    - **Benchmark with other similar sports packages:** Research what other clubs are charging for a similar package to your organisation.
    - **Media valuation:** What is the media value that will be obtained from the sponsorship? This may require a professional agency to evaluate your package and to identify a media value.

4. **Create a sales presentation:** A sales presentation allows you to tell your story and outline the opportunity to a potential sponsor. A sales presentation shows a sponsor that you are serious and professional in your approach. The sponsorship sales presentation should be tailored for each sponsor and should cover:
    - Information about your club, including the number of members, key achievements, competitions you are involved in, digital reach etc.
    - The benefits to their business of taking this sponsorship opportunity, including:
        - Driving sales and revenue to their premises
        - Generating positive public relations (PR) for their business
        - Supporting an area of the club that fits with the business values, i.e. women's sport
            - Seek to solve their challenges or issues
    - Aligning the profile of people who attend your club to that of the business customer profile. Know your player and fanbase demographics. Businesses sponsoring grassroots clubs must know they'll reach their desired audience.
    - Linking their business values and objectives to your club values and objectives. If you can find a link between your club and their brand, you'll find it easier to pitch the value of being involved with your club.

- The potential publicity from media coverage, traditional media and online.
- List of packages or sponsorship opportunities available.
- The reasons why they should partner with your club. Emphasise your relevance and reach within the community.
- Showcase the details of any other sponsors you currently work with.
- Your contact details.

REMEMBER

Obtain photographs and media coverage of any PR coverage which includes the sponsor's logo. Collect these in a folder and ensure that the business receives copies.

Be sure to invite representatives of the sponsor to your events throughout the year.

THINK!

Why not set up a 'business membership' in your club where each organisation that joins recieves benefits (networking events, social media coverage, website/member promotion) in return for an annual fee?

5. **Identify a list of businesses to target:** The income generation committee should create a spreadsheet (possibly in Microsoft Excel) of potential businesses to target. This should include:
    - Identifying club members, coaches and players who are business owners who can introduce the income generation committee to their network of business contacts – you might suggest that they possibly introduce you to five businesses per person.
    - Conduct an audit of your youth and adult players. Does any parent or player own a business or hold a senior position in a business? Can you approach them about becoming involved as a sponsor?
    - Attend local business and community events to meet people and find potential sponsors. For example, local mortgage brokers, energy providers, local garages, greengrocers, butchers, estate agents and solicitors.

    The spreadsheet should include the following data:
    - Contact name
    - Business name

- Position
- Contact mobile number
- Contact email address
- Date contacted
- Likely interest in sponsorship (Y/N)

Use the template shown in Figure 9.3 to create your own sponsors target list:

Contact Name	Business Name	Position	Phone Number	Email Address	Date Contacted	key contact in the club	Interested (Y/N)
Sam Wilson	ABC Ltd	Director	0123 456 789	sam@mybusiness.com	1/12/20xx	George Hay	Yes. Set up meeting in next 2 weeks

Figure 9.3 Target sponsors list

> You can find a blank copy of the "Sponsors Target List" template in the appendix.

6. **Go sell:** In a grassroots club, split the list between the members of the income generation committee. The committee members should be given some basic training on sales and how to give a presentation. It is important to provide committee members with sales training. In some cases, in-kind support might be as valuable as a financial contribution. In all cases, the sales presentation should be used when meeting potential sponsors.

The key is to gain a personal introduction from someone within the club.

REMEMBER

It is important that the club understands the objectives of the business they are trying to secure sponsorship from. When the club is seeking a sponsor, it should research the short, medium and long-term objectives of the potential sponsor and make sure that the package matches the objectives of the business.

The research should include the profile of their customers, marketing messages, values and keywords on their website.

Create an authentic long-term partnership built on trust.

7. **Sign a contract, letter of agreement:** All sponsorship agreements should have a contract or at least a signed letter of agreement. If this is not possible, a detailed email will suffice at grassroots level. Make sure to include:
   - Payment amounts
   - Contract duration and dates
   - List of the rights obtained
   - Obligations of both parties
   - Whether or not the agreement is exclusive, giving details of category exclusivity, if applicable
   - Termination clauses
   - Key contacts
   - Framework and options on renewal

   Grassroots clubs can outline the agreement in an email or one-page document, which clearly sets out what has been agreed between the sponsor and the club.

   A nice touch is to send a letter of thanks from club chair to the business owner.

8. **Hold a kick-off meeting:** It is recommended to hold a kick-off meeting with the sponsor to clearly define their objectives and to start planning an event calendar for the season ahead. The kick-off meeting should be held shortly after signing the contract or agreement. This is an important meeting, as it clearly sets out the sponsors' objectives, outlines future meeting dates and ensures a smooth start to the relationship.

9. **Account management:** Ensure that you meet the sponsors every month or quarter to discuss the following:
   - Reviewing sponsors' objectives and ensuring whether they are being met
   - Awareness or coverage in the local media from the previous month
   - Up-and-coming communications with your members, i.e. possible sponsor's offers, forthcoming club events etc.
   - Dealing with any issues or concerns that the sponsor may have
   - Considering future joint campaigns

   Regular check-ins with your sponsors are essential.

10. **Final review meeting:** This will come towards the end of the agreement. This meeting should reflect on whether the sponsors' objectives have been met. If not, why? Is the sponsor keen to renew? How can the partnership be improved?

Tip: Conduct an annual online survey aimed at your players, parents, spectators and coaches. Ask questions such as:

- Are you aware of (insert business name) sponsoring our club?
- Are you more likely to support (insert business name) due to their involvement with our club?
- Rate your feelings about (insert business name) on a scale of 1–10.
- Do you feel more positive about (insert business name) due to their involvement in our club? Are you more likely to buy their product/service due to their involvement in our club?

Securing Sponsorship

- **Branding:** Sponsors want to be associated with a partner who has a positive image. So spend time building your brand and image in your community.
- **Reach:** Build up your reach in the community. This can be achieved through connecting with more adults, ensuring a strong youth structure in place and by expanding your online presence. Many sponsors will want to know the reach you have. The bigger the reach, the more opportunities exist for them.
- **Expertise:** What expertise does the sponsor have which can benefit the club i.e. marketing, financial etc.?
- **People:** During the sales presentation stage, ensure that you are dealing with the decision maker in the business.
- **Relationship:** Ensure that dialogue remains open so that the sponsor has the opportunity to continue investing in your club once their initial contract expires. A strong relationship can be achieved by maintaining frequent communication.

How to Keep a Sponsor

- There should be regular communication between the sponsor and the club. This could be weekly, monthly or quarterly. Areas to discuss include latest announcements, joint campaigns, media and social activity and community programmes. Ensure the sponsor sees the value in the partnership in terms of sales generated, media and digital coverage and links into the community.
- Build relationships between all your sponsors. Create an annual sponsors workshop (exchange club information and identify areas of potential collaboration).
- Have one person responsible for the relationship between the sponsor and the club.

Grants and Foundations

Many governments or foundations offer grants to community-based organisations. These grants can be either capital (building a new clubhouse, development of a pitch or court etc.) or programme-related grants (coaching or educational programmes in the local community).

These grants and foundations can be an interesting income stream but require a definite plan and commitment to see them through to successful implementation.

Grants and foundations can come in a range of different ways:

- City and local government/region
- National government/province
- Business and community foundations

Visit your local 'grant finder' website to identify potential grants.

> You can find a copy of the "Grant Identification" template in the appendix.

City and Local Government/Region

Your local city or regional government will offer a variety of sporting and community grants. There are a range of grants available concerning different areas of your club:

- Facility development
- Programme costs
- Training and development
- Community programmes
- Equipment

As a club, it is important to focus on sports development and **consider community and health grants.**

It is important to 'not chase the money'; refer to your club development plan and see what grants and foundations can help you achieve your objectives.

THINK

Develop relationships throughout the year with potential grant providers, not just when a grant programme is being made available.

Unsuccessful Grant Applications

Why are applications unsuccessful?

This may be due to a number of reasons, including:

- The application does not meet the grant criteria.
- Not enough time has been spent on researching the issue or problem.
- Applicants fail to illustrate why their project is essential.
- The project is poorly planned and there is no indication of where the funding will be spent.

DEVELOPING QUALITY APPLICATIONS

There is no right or wrong way to make a grant application but it is possible to increase your club's chances of successfully securing a grant by taking the following into account:

- Conduct research with your members and in your local area/community. Identify what is required within your community and how you can solve that need through your project. Research can be conducted through online surveys and/or through a number of focus groups.
- The stronger the reach and community impact, the greater the chance the proposal will receive serious consideration.
- Ensure your project is well planned. What are the objectives? What is the project trying to achieve? Illustrate how the project will make a difference in your community.
- Outline when and where your project is going to take place.
- Accurately cost your project.
- Provide evidence of good management on the project team. Who is responsible for the project in your club?
- Provide supporting evidence such as recent bank statements, club development plans, letters of support from local politicians, club constitution, your recent annual report and audited financial accounts.

National Government/Province

Grants from the national government can be secured from a wide range of departments, such as the departments of education, health and community relations, to name but a few.

Tips when applying for government funding:

- Ensure you have read the 'programme for government' documentation, which sets out their key objectives. When applying for funding, ensure your application meets their key performance indicators (KPIs).
- Conduct a review of all the potential grants available in your area from national government.
- Conduct research into other sports clubs that have been successful in securing government funding from a range of different schemes.
- Ensure that you don't chase the money. The funding secured must be linked to your club development plan.

Business and Community Foundations

Many corporate organisations and community foundations exist. There can be a good supply of grant funding for clubs for various sports and community programmes and infrastructure projects.

Clubs should research into the business and community foundations available in your area.

Following the research, the criteria for each foundation should be reviewed, as you may not be able to apply for certain grants based on the criteria set.

Use the template shown in Figure 9.4 to identify a wide range of government and foundation grants open to your club.

List the varioius community, foundations, local and national government grants	Do you meet the criteria? Y/N	How much funding can be secured? £	What can the funding be used for in the club - capital / infrastructure, programmes, equipment, etc?
Supermarket foundation	Yes	5,000	Coach education busary's

Figure 9.4 Government and foundation grant template

> You can find a blank copy of the "Grant Identification" template in the appendix.

Applying for Grants

General guidelines for all grant types include:

❖ The best way to navigate the world of grants is to consider your needs before you start thinking about what's available.

❖ Hold a brainstorming session for all club members, making a list of all that your group would like to do, if only it had the money. Make it a living list that is accessible to key people within the organisation; one can be added to, and refined, as new needs arise and old ones subside. Use this list to inform your decisions about which grants you want to apply for.

❖ Grant making is personal. The more a funder knows about your club, the more likely you are to receive funding. Likewise, the more you know about a funder, the better you can tailor your application to meet their values and interests.

❖ Don't be afraid to reach out to a funder and have a meeting with their funding team, in order to cultivate a relationship; unless they specifically say not to, always push for a face-to face meeting.

- It is important to be relevant to the funder and provide them with evidence of why your club needs their funds, and the benefits that their help would bring.
- Establish a specific need in the geographical area and prove how your club will realistically address this.
- It is all about building and cultivating an ongoing and meaningful relationship. Honest, transparent and responsible behaviour will help you achieve your aim.
- Groups that provide a positive impact on the locality will attract and retain grantors and supporters, due to the good reputation they build. Having an impressive reputation locally, while maintaining strong relationships, will make it easier to obtain funding next time.

TIPS

Can you secure a grant by organising the following?

- A grassroots festival with a focus on keeping kids fit and healthy
- A programme to reach out to various communities in your area
- A range of educational seminars or workshops to train your volunteers

TIP

It is advised that you talk with a successful applicant to gain an understanding of what detail must go into the application.

Club Facilities (Club Shop, Rental of Rooms, Bar Sales)

Clubs either own or rent their own club house or venue. In certain cases, managing a facility can bring potential revenue opportunities.

This may include:

- Rental of the court, 3G or grass pitch to other clubs for training and games (providing the club owns the facility)
- A bar for food and beverage sales
- Establishing a shop or kiosk to sell club-branded merchandise
- Rental of rooms for businesses in local areas as office space
- Utilising the car park for events, such as a car boot sale

THINK

Conduct research with other sports clubs in terms of how they generate income from their facility.

Donations/Patronage

Donations can come from various sources, from wealthy individuals connected with the club, to the surrounding community or from a range of individuals who donate a smaller fee per person. Patronage is ongoing financial aid or support from an individual or collective group.

If you are fortunate to secure a donation or patronage, it is important to identify:

- Are there any specifications linked to the donation? For example, the money can only be spent on youth programmes?
- Is the donor looking for something in return, i.e. a seat on the board or committee?
- Is the donation a one-off or an annual contribution?

REMEMBER

Make sure to send a letter of thanks on behalf of the club to the donor or patron.

Online/Digital Revenue

Generating income from online platforms is a growth area for sports clubs. The following outlines the key digital revenue opportunities:

a. Digital advertising or sponsorship on the club's website/email/app and other online platforms, such as YouTube
b. Online shop on the club's website and other eCommerce platforms such as Amazon
c. Online membership (player registration) through the club's website
d. Sponsored content on your social media sites. For example, goal of the week, save of the week, etc. brought to you by a specific sponsor
e. Online lottery, last man standing, raffle or prize draws via online websites
f. Online betting, with a commission going to the club
g. Online ticket sales on the club's website (especially for semi-professional clubs) (This also includes selling VIP hospitality packages online.)
h. Crowdfunding – where you harness the internet to ask 'friends' to donate a fee to a specific cause

The above list is not exhaustive but gives a flavour of where income can be driven online (see Figure 9.5).

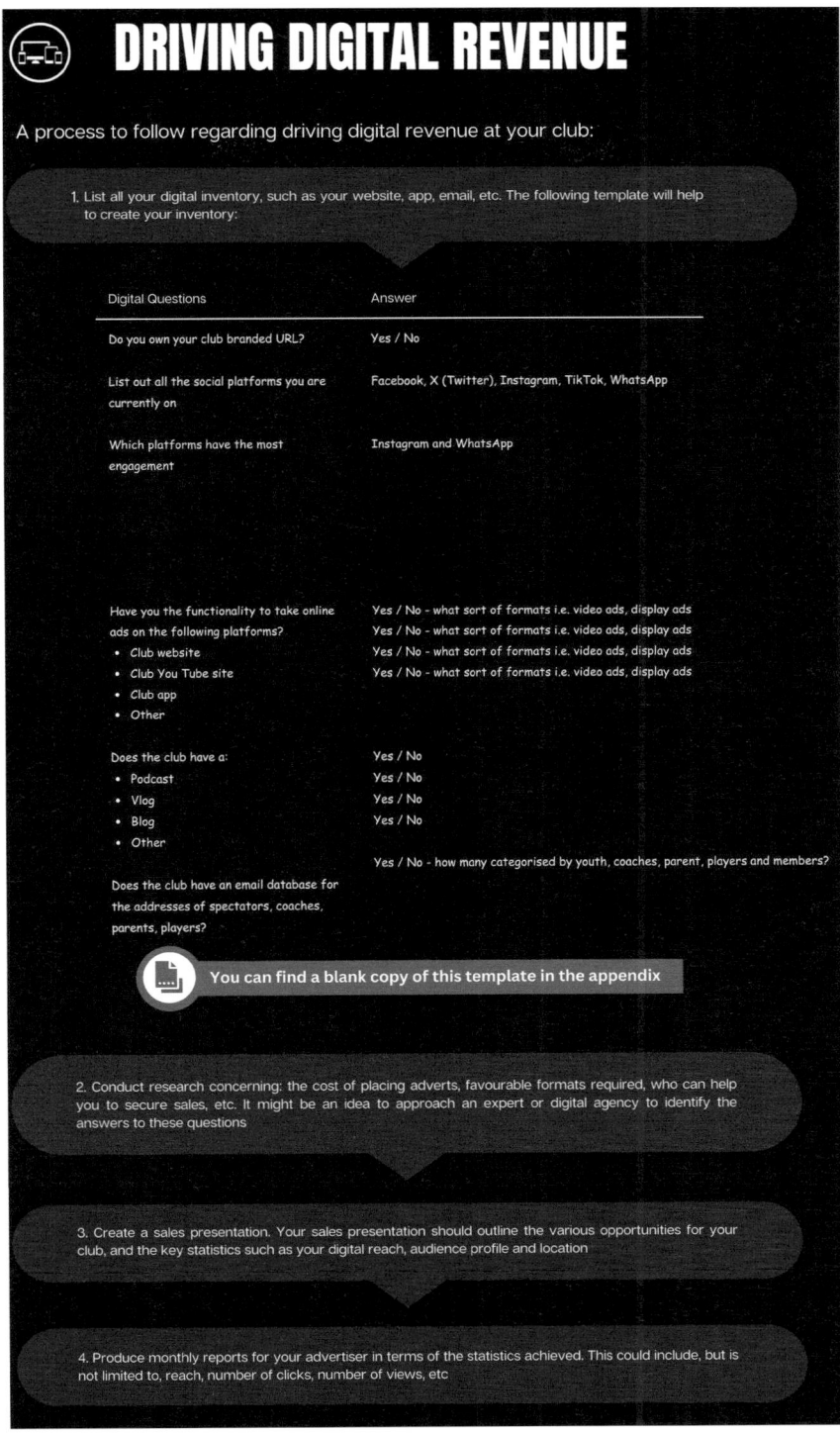

Figure 9.5 Process for identifying digital revenue

Holiday Camps

Organising holiday camps is an interesting way to generate income for your club.

Holiday camps can be organised during the summer, at Christmas, Easter or other times when children are off school.

Income from holiday camps can be generated from the following areas:

- **Registration fee:** A parent pays for the child to be enrolled on the camp.
- **Food and beverage sales:** The child and/or the parent can purchase a range of food and beverages during the camp.
- **Sponsorship:** A business decides to become the sponsor of the camp in exchange for naming rights and other benefits agreed with the club.
- **Merchandise:** Kids can purchase club-branded products during the camp.

It takes a lot of efforts to organise a successful holiday camp.

A club should consider the following before embarking on a holiday camp programme:

1. **Availability and quality of coaches:** Have you the right number and quality of coaches available for each day of the camp? Have they been through a child safeguarding course? Have they created a daily programme of activity? Are the days fully planned out from a coaching viewpoint?
2. **Facility:** Have you confirmed the availability of pitches during the camp days?
3. **Costs:** Have you clearly identified all the costs associated with running a holiday camp? For example,
    - Rent of facility/pitch/court
    - Marketing and promotional costs
    - Coaching fees
    - Food and beverage costs
    - Public liability insurance
    - Equipment – balls, bibs, cones etc.
4. **Income:** Have you identified all the income streams associated with the camps? Are you making profit? Will you be taking registrations online? What system will you be using? Have you briefed the income generation committee to assist in securing a sponsor?
5. **Marketing and promotions:** Have you considered the marketing and promotional activity required to generate the numbers? Consider sending flyers to the local schools, parents of your youth players, promotion on social media, erecting posters in local community areas, articles in your local newspaper etc. Have you briefed your communications committee?

Used with permission from Shutterstock/PeopleImages.com - Yuri A.

Organise events throughout the year to drive income for your club.

Ticketing

Not every club is able to charge a fee for its home games or events. A lot of things depend on the structure of the ground/facility and the league in which the game is played. Is the venue in an open public space or is it a private facility surrounded by fencing, with turnstiles?

If you play your home games in a public facility, ticketing is unlikely to be an option. Rather, a simple bucket collection may be an alternative.

Ticketing is an option for clubs with the appropriate facility or stadium. The key elements to consider regarding ticketing include:

- ❖ **Setting the price:** This might be based on ticket prices set by the league or other clubs in your surrounding area. It might be based on the ticketing income you need to achieve and your income generation plan. Price can also be subject to change, depending on the standard of facility and the entertainment offered
- ❖ **Promotion:** How are you informing the community of your ticket availability? A major part of this will be your reach into the community and to your members. This will cover your club website, social media platforms, email database, app etc. It is important to ensure that you use the same creative image and message across all your marketing platforms.

- **Sales outlets:** Are you selling the tickets online, at your club on game day, via sponsors or other community outlets? Are you using a ticketing provider to sell tickets or are you doing this yourself?
- **Ticket packages:** Are you offering a range of packages to suit your community/spectator base, i.e. season ticket, single or family ticket prices, children, old age pensioners (OAPs) or those with a disability?

> ## TICKET PRICING
> There are many factors that can affect the pricing of tickets, including:
>
> - Your current league position
> - The quality of the opponent (i.e. a local derby, game against the league leaders)
> - Whether it is a league or cup game
> - The quality of the entertainment you offer to attendees before the game, at half-time and post-game
> - The standard of your facility

Used with permission from Shutterstock/bodrumsurf.

Merchandise

Developing a merchandising range requires time and some investment but the benefits to the club can go beyond the simple ability to generate revenue through sales:

1. It provides value to sponsors by having their logo on the club merchandise (tracksuits, polo tops etc.).
2. It can give your club a presence in the local community when players and members wear the product.

The following process should be applied when embarking on a merchandising programme for your club:

- Gather research from your members in terms of interest in purchasing a range of club-branded products.
- Identify potential sports apparel providers who will supply a range of products identified from the research.
- Source a design drawing of the range and a sample for the members to view (consider your club colour, logo and club motto when designing the product range).
- Select the sports apparel provider. This could be based on price, delivery, quality of product, etc. (ensure that the business can take online orders and agree process for returning products). Quality is extremely important as it ensures member satisfaction and lasting wear.
- Gather the orders and money from the members, players and parents.
- Place the order.
- Arrange a delivery date with the club members, players and parents to collect the products.
- Go live with the online shop ordering facility via the sports apparel partner.
- Promote the online shop on the club's website and social media channels.
- Track merchandise sales on a monthly or quarterly basis.

Note: Milestone anniversaries for the club can be celebrated with an entirely new kit or leisure range which can also be sold to spectators and supporters of the club.

THINK

Make it easy for customers to purchase products either directly or online and ensure you have a range of sizes available for members.

Other Sources

Several other income streams can exist for a club. These include:

A. **Cup winnings:** Businesses sponsor a number of league and cup competitions. Winning a cup tournament, or getting to the final stages of the tournament, can generate additional revenue for the club, depending on your final position in the competition. In addition, some competitions provide a revenue split of the gate income.
B. **Reduction in costs by securing in-kind support:** While this is not an income stream per se, keeping a handle on your costs and securing in-kind support from local individuals or members will help to save costs for the club. This might involve anything from joinery work to cleaning the club house.
C. **Game fees:** In some clubs, a 'game fee' is also charged to players. This fee usually covers the referee's fee or otherwise goes into a club kitty.

Final Thought

In this chapter, we examined various income streams available to grassroots clubs, highlighting opportunities for financial growth and sustainability. The next step for your club is to meet and identify the key income streams that align with your goals, as well as to develop clear annual targets for the duration of your club plan. Looking ahead, the next chapter will shift our focus to facilities and how they impact your club's overall success and community engagement.

Used with permission from Shutterstock/Wirestock Creators.

10

Facilities
Making the most of the club's facilities

All clubs need facilities to play, whether comprising a rented pitch/court or a facility with multiple pitches, with a club house. It can be challenging to manage facilities and coordinate on-pitch/court activities, social occasion, registrations and everything else that a club needs to offer.

High-standard sports facilities are not currently available to all members of grassroots level clubs though. Far from it, field lighting, poor quality playing of surfaces, a shortage of equipment, poor drainage etc. are some of the common issues that clubs deal with on a seasonal basis.

This chapter aims to provide clubs with ideas and guidance on addressing deficiencies in a facility and work with their governing body to address them. It also outlines what supports are available and how best to maintain your facility.

> This chapter focuses on the following areas:
>
> 1. How to manage your facility
> 2. How to maintain your facility

Things to Consider

- ❖ Keep on top of the maintenance
- ❖ Protect your property from vandals and burglars
- ❖ Prepare for any emergencies, such as fire

> Priority areas to adopt in your club after reading this chapter:
>
> 1. Create a facility management plan
> 2. Create a facility maintenance plan
> 3. Access all possible grants pertaining to facilities

Owning or Leasing a Facility

Clubs have two options when it comes to facilities:

Rental or leasing of the facility from a third party such as the local government or land owner
Ownership of the facility (often this is the most expensive solution as you will probably need to secure substantial funding to develop your own facilities. You will also need to seek planning consent and meet the ongoing costs associated with owning any premises.)

The option you take will depend on many different factors such as:

- Funding to purchase land
- Availability of land in your local community
- Strategic intent to own and operate the facility

If you own your own facility, you must maintain and ensure the property is fit for sport each season.

It is the responsibility of sports clubs to provide adequate spaces to play and to ensure sufficient facilities to meet the growing demand. That requires a robust strategy of maintaining quality playing fields, developing new playing surfaces, managing existing infrastructure and establishing new facilities.

Clubs need to keep facilities up-to-date. You should have a plan regarding who maintains the club facility and who is responsible for facility planning. If you are developing a facility, you need to know the best practices in this regard.

Relationships with Your Local Council

Clubs need to have first-hand knowledge of key personnel at local council who can help with all matters relating to your facilities. Maintaining a close relationship with your local council member will increase your chances of obtaining grant funding and engagement within your community. In Chapter 9, we spoke about income generation, and relationships with local government, in that regard. You need to determine your contacts at local, state and national government.

Building Relationships with the Council

- Find out the name of your local councillor and invite them to a club event or to attend a game.
- Share a copy of your club development plan with the councillor and include a letter, specifying your goals.
- Understand where and how the relationship with the council is important to your club – Do they provide the facilities you use? Do they provide cleaning or other services? Do you pay them rates? etc.

- Research their supports and how and where those supports could be useful to your club; understand what their grant application process is and what the deadlines are.
- Find out if any of your club members have experience in dealing with the council, applying for grants etc.
- Include the council officers in your email and newsletter updates.
- Seek a formal meeting, where you can outline plans for the club, moving forward.
- Formally follow up with a letter, specifying your plans and intentions to work together.

Facilities Audit

In terms of your club, you should also undertake a regular facility and equipment audit. This audit will help identify where equipment is missing/broken/no longer fit for purpose, and map out your current and future needs. Your overall goal in terms of a facilities audit should be the continual improvement of the player experience in a safe and conducive environment. Your audit might identify the need to improve the quality of a playing field/court, provide floodlights that allow night games and additional training or the development of changing-room facilities that cater for both men and women.

Key steps in a facilities audit are:

- A data-collection process – to create an inventory of what you have. Decide first exactly what will be included on the audit, e.g. sporting equipment only or also including canteen crockery, for example.
- Decide who is collecting this data.
- Establish what baseline information you will have on your audit. Will you measure the number of items? What condition are they in? What is the location? What is the make/model? When is it next due for service? Who is responsible for it? etc.
- Include buildings, grounds and equipment.
- Aim to complete the audit from start to finish, within a short-given timeframe, e.g. two weeks.

As a minimum, the audit should record the following:

- Outline the facilities (stands, club house, pitch, court etc.)
- Quality and size
- Where the facility is located
- Age of each facility
- Condition of each facility
- Is the facility in good working order/issues?
- Does the facility meet the needs of the users/identify the current and future needs based on member demographics and usage patterns?

- ❖ Has the facility been repaired recently? When?
- ❖ Evidence of future needs/repairs
- ❖ Estimated remaining lifetime of the facility
- ❖ Costs required to upgrade, maintain or replace the facility
- ❖ Identify potential funding options such as government grants, community fund-raising etc.

Figure 10.1 shows a facility plan template.

FACILITY PLAN EXAMPLE

Facility area	Work required	Actions required	Owner	Deadline	Budget
Baseball Court	New court in required	Approach potential suppliers, confirm budget, raise funds etc	George McLeary	31 July 202x	$50,000
Changing rooms	Painting of both changing rooms	Agree colours, purchase the paint, approach volunteers and agree date for painting	Leanne McCrory	31 Sept 202x	$500
etc					

Figure 10.1 Facility plan template

> You can find a blank copy of the "Facility Plan" template in the appendix.

Facility Usage

It is often a constant battle for club administrators to organise and allocate pitches and any indoor facilities for teams and/or individuals to train. Sometimes the availability of space and equipment for training does not match the number of people who need to use it. In developing a facility management plan, club administrators must consider what is feasible with regard to the use of pitches and facilities, and try to determine whether there is a 'membership ceiling', above which problems become impossible to solve without investing in further facilities. If there are inadequate training facilities, it will have a detrimental effect on the membership. Furthermore, overuse of facilities will cause a degradation in the quality of programmes.

A facility-use schedule is an important component of a club's facility management plan for managing the facility. See this sample facility usage schedule template in Figure 10.2.

Team Name	Age Group	Day	Time	Venue Location (Training)	Lead Coach
Example FC	Under-12	Monday	19.00 to 20:00	London Park	Sam Wilson

Figure 10.2 Facility usage schedule template

> You can find a blank copy of the "Facility Usage Schedule" template in the appendix.

Facilities Management Plan

A facilities management plan, sometimes referred to as a strategic facility plan, or facility master plan, is a document that describes an organisation's facilities, alongside their purpose and plans for the future. It outlines how the facilities will be utilised following the organisation's business plan. It is also a way to inform others of current activities, where the club is headed, and how it expects to get there.

> **WHAT SHOULD BE INCLUDED IN A FACILITY MANAGEMENT PLAN?**
>
> ❖ General information about your club
> ❖ How well your existing facilities match your membership and usage
> ❖ Recommendations for future actions that will enhance your facilities
> ❖ How those facilities will be managed and funded
> ❖ How better facilities will integrate into, and support, your local community, e.g. shared usage of an indoor space with a pensioners' club

Strategic Facility Plan

Here are your seven simple steps for creating a strategic facility plan:

1. **Identify the necessary facilities for your organisation:** The first step is to identify what facilities are necessary and appropriate for your club. Details of all existing facilities (pitches/courts, clubhouse, lock-up etc.) as well as recommendations for any new facilities or expansions for current facilities should be provided.
2. **Explain why you need them and where they should be located:** Projected pitch and facility usage is essential in facility master plans as they allow stakeholders (local authorities, grant givers etc.) to understand the specific needs of the club. Location of the facilities is important as that can impact other factors, e.g. will a new pitch take up what was previously a parking lot, thereby displacing cars?
3. **Explore the value of the facilities to your Club and community:** Facilities bring value to a club and a community – not just by increasing club activity but also by improving the overall attractiveness and image of a community and other social returns such as improved health, less delinquency etc. A detailed list of all values (along with anticipated monetary values or growth percentages, where appropriate) should be documented.
4. **Identify required inventory and equipment:** Some facilities will require considerable expense in order to fully equip them to a club's needs. Take your time identifying all potential costs, both to get the facility up and running for the long-term. The more accurate your costings, the more effective your plan will become.
5. **Write up the document:** Once you have gathered all of the above information together, it should be written up into a formal report. Usually, strategic facility plans follow a structure similar to the following:
   - Executive summary
   - Introduction
   - Facility recommendations
   - Workforce analysis (if relevant)
   - Site inventory
   - Recommendations
   - Approvals and sign-off
   - Appendices
6. **Get management approval:** The completed plan must be approved by the club board and any relevant stakeholders. You should allow them time to read the report thoroughly and complete any amendments that they require. Provide space near the end of the report for sign-off signatures and dates to be written in.

7. **Distribute the document and refer to it regularly:** It's important to distribute the plan to your key stakeholders and club members so that they have easy access to it. The facility master plan must be referred to regularly in order to be effective. If changes in your club occur that would change the outcomes of the plan, it should be amended and a new version circulated.

Facilities Maintenance

The key facilities requiring maintenance are:

Clearly and Accurately Mark out the Field or Court

Consideration also needs to be given to pitch and grass recovery and maintenance, and a schedule should be in place for watering, cutting, regrowth and general pitch maintenance, where the council does not provide that.

In the case of multi-use games area (MUGA) or synthetic (3G/4G) pitches, an ongoing maintenance schedule and contract should be in place with the pitch provider, who will be an expert in maintaining that type of pitch.

Lighting

Adequate lighting for sports fields or venue is now an essential element in the ongoing viability of any venue. While community football clubs are unlikely to need the standard of lighting required for televised games, nearly all clubs need to be able to light their grounds so that players of all ages can train safely and effectively at night, or even late afternoon in winter.

Toilet Facility

Your club should always ensure that both the public and disabled toilets are clean and available for members and guests. These toilets should be signposted and stocked with hand towels and toilet paper.

Changing Rooms

Changing rooms provide an important first impression for members, especially senior teams, who tend to use these rooms more than juniors and underage players (although younger players often use the changing rooms during camps). Clean and presentable changing rooms provide players comfort and give a positive impression of your club to both members and visiting teams.

Changing rooms are a key area for team bonding pre/post games. Therefore, sufficient space is provided for the full team, giving them a place to focus on the game ahead together. Posters or motivational signage up on walls of the changing room, and the facility to play music, might also be appropriate.

> **THINK!**
>
> Check your smoke/fire and alarm systems are working on an annual basis.

> **THINK!**
>
> Set aside a pot of money for maintenance and upgrading your facility each season.

Used with permission from Shutterstock/Andrew Angelov.

> **REMEMBER**
>
> All sporting equipment, whether fixed or portable, large or small, must be properly secured and anchored, and are stable and safe for use at all times and make sure your facilities adhere to local building codes, safety standards and accessibility regulations.

> **THINK**
>
> Can you reduce costs by installing solar panels or LED lights at the club?

Insurance

Insurance can be challenging for sports clubs and is expensive, so it is worth considering carefully what insurance you might need.

Even if you only want the bare minimum coverage for your club, you'll need liability insurance. General liability insurance typically covers your legal costs and damages from any lawsuit dealing with injury and property damage caused directly or indirectly by your club. General liability policies vary significantly, so you will need to read the fine print for any policy you consider. In addition to physical injury and property damage, your liability policy may also cover lawsuits related to things like personal injury, sexual abuse and directors' insurance.

Many clubs also choose to insure their property from theft and damage. Property and equipment insurance might include coverage for weather-related damage to your outdoor equipment, such as bleachers and scoreboards, general accidental damage to your indoor equipment, such as your turf and pitching machines, or even damage to your building (such as that caused by a fire, flood, tornado or vandalism). Of course, the cost and options for equipment and property insurance will depend on its value and the risks it faces. You can discuss all those details and options with your agent or broker.

You may also need a team policy, which typically covers every player on a team for practices, games and tournaments, wherever they play. You may want to look for coverage that isn't limited to sport but that covers every team event (parties, picnics, banquets etc.).

Final Thought

In this final chapter, we centred on facility development and maintenance, emphasising the importance of conducting a thorough audit and creating a comprehensive facilities plan. This process will help identify current strengths and areas for improvement, ensuring your club's facilities meet the needs of members and community. Your club can enhance its functionality and appeal by prioritizing effective development and maintenance.

THINK!

Check what you're already insured for (premises and equipment) and what you need to get insurance for.

REMEMBER

- Always have a first-aid kit on site.
- If possible, have a defibrillator on site.

Used with permission from Shutterstock/Juice Dash.

Appendix
Templates and Checklists

Club Development Framework Model

For amateur (recreational/community) or semi-professional clubs.

Visit https://geoffwnjwilson.com/2024/01/30/club-development-framework-model-for-the-sports-industry/ for additional information on the model.

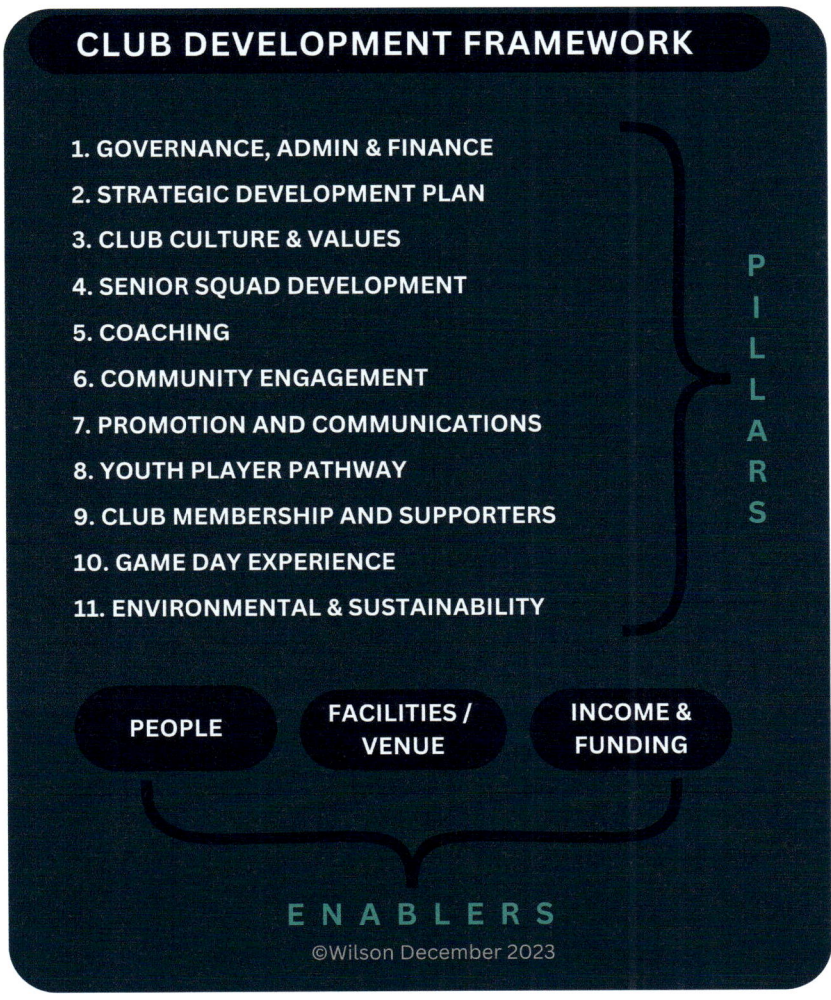

Is This Guide for You?

	YES	NO
Has a club development plan been created & approved by the board?		
Do you have a modern and recently up-to-date club constitution?		
Do you have active committees (action oriented committees who meet regularly)?		
Have you appointed capable and skilled individuals in key roles; chairperson, secretary, treasurer, safeguarding officer, public relations officer, youth/academy/technical director (the number of roles depends on the size of your club)?		
Have you clearly defined roles and responsibilities for the staff/volunteers?		
Do you have robust financial procedures in place – from annual budget setting to monthly or quarterly income and expenditure accounts?		
Do you communicate with members and key stakeholders on a regular basis (i.e. face to face meetings with parents, coaches, players, fans, local councils etc.)?		
Do you provide ongoing training of staff or volunteers each year, i.e. coach education workshops, good governance, safeguarding training?		

If you have placed a tick in the NO column in the majority of the areas, then this handbook is for you!

Action Log List

See Chapter 1 of the handbook for more details.

Action Number	Action	Person Responsible	Completion date	Status (not started, in progress, completed)

Checklist of Policies

See Chapter 1 of the handbook for more details	☑
Child protection	☐
Safeguarding policy	☐
Data protection policy	☐
Equality & diversity policy	☐
Conflict of interest	☐
Recruitment policy	☐
Disciplinary policy	☐
Code of conduct for parents, spectators, volunteers, committee/club officials coaches & players	☐
Anti-bullying policy	☐
Dispute resolution	☐

Date checklist reviewed: _____

Name of person: _____

Safeguarding Checklist

See Chapter 1 of the handbook for more details.

The following is a useful checklist to use when reviewing safeguarding in your club:

Safeguarding policy	Y	N
Does your club have a safeguarding policy for the protection of children/young people/vulnerable adults?	☐	☐
Designated safeguarding officer		
Do you have a designated safeguarding officer responsible for all issues regarding the protection of children, young people and vulnerable adults?	☐	☐
Codes of conduct/behavior		
Do you have written standards of good practice i.e. a code of conduct/behaviour?	☐	☐
Do you have a process to ensure that the code of conduct/behaviour is communicated to relevant parties – volunteers/staff/parents/young people so they are aware of the standards set by your club?	☐	☐
Training		
Do you ensure that your volunteers have access to appropriate safeguarding training? [Note: It is a good practice to keep a record of those volunteers/staff who have attended safeguarding training.]	☐	☐
Reporting		
Do you have procedures for dealing with complaints and concerns regarding poor practice, abuse or neglect i.e. clear reporting procedures?	☐	☐
Recruitment		
Do you have recruitment procedures for those working/volunteering with young people that include:	☐	☐
❖ Completing an information/application form that enables the applicant to self-declare any previous offences; and	☐	☐
❖ Completing a police check (or equivalent) for those working with or responsible for children or young people (i.e. regulated positions)	☐	☐

Date checklist reviewed: _____

Name of person: _____

Accident Report Form

See Chapters 1 and 8 of the handbook for more details.

Club details	
Name of club	
Coach in attendance	
Injured party details	
Name	
Home address	
Accident details	
Form completed by	
Date/Time	
Exact location	
Time reported	
Reported by who	
Nature of injury	
How accident happened	
Name/Contact details of witnesses	
First aid involved (Y/N)	
Were the following contacted:	☐ Police ☐ Ambulance
Parents involved (Y/N)	
By whom?	
When?	

Emergency Details Form

See Chapters 1 and 8 of this handbook for more details.

Club details	
Name of club	
Name(s) of coach(es)	
Team/age group	
Venue	

Participant name	Address	DOB	Important medical information	Emergency contact name	Relationship to participant	Contact number

Conflict of Interest Register

See Chapter 1 of the handbook for more details.

Name of person in the club	Position in the club	Person and / or Organisation With Interest	Nature of Conflict of Interest	Date of Declaration

Risk Register

See Chapter 1 of the handbook for more details.

Risk number	Description of the risk	Likelihood of risk happening (1-5)*	Impact of the risk (1-5)*	Controls / Mitigation	Owner

*1 is highly unlikely, 2 is unlikely 3 is moderate/possible, 4 is likely and 5 is highly likely

Pre-development Plan Checklist

See Chapter 2 of the handbook for more details.

Use the checklist below before you start the process of creating your development plan

	YES	NO
Are you affiliated with your governing body?		
Are your board members up for re-election soon? (It is not good practice to start the development plan process when the chair and board members are up for re-election or are about to step down from the board)		
Have you elected a club development plan committee and project leader?(A committee that will oversee the development and implementation of the plan)		
Have you a committee structure in place? Consider committees covering areas such as youth development, income generation, communication etc. This is important as it will be these committees which will help you implement the plan.		
Do you produce an annual budget?		
Do you produce monthly or quarterly income and expenditure accounts?		
Do you have a robust income generation plan in place to raise money for the club?		
Do you have sufficient volunteers and coaches to help you run the club?		

If you have answered NO to the majority of the above, it is recommended that you consider actioning these areas before embarking on creating your club development plan.

This will give you a solid foundation from which to create your plan.

Club Development Plan

See Chapter 2 of the handbook for more details.

The following template can be used by your club:

Outline the results of your research (situational analysis, 1:1s, focus groups and surveys)
Notes ❖
Outline the vision, mission and value definition of the club
Notes ❖
Outline the key goals
Notes 1. 2. 3.
The key objectives under each goal*

Goal:

Objective	Key Actions (list the key tasks under each obj)	Completion Date (acheived by)	Responsibility (who is the owner)	KPI/Measure (Target)	W.R.A.G. (is it on schedule)

Goal:

Objective	Key Actions (list the key tasks under each obj)	Completion Date (acheived by)	Responsibility (who is the owner)	KPI/Measure (Target)	W.R.A.G. (is it on schedule)

*Add in additional tables for each individual goal

The plan will be monitored throughout the year
Notes ❖
People & finances
Notes ❖

SWOT Analysis

See Chapter 2 of the handbook for more details.

Strengths	Weaknesses	Opportunities	Threats

Stakeholder Analysis

See Chapter 2 of the handbook for more details.

Stakeholder or stakeholder group	How the club currently engages and communicates with stakeholders?	What is the current relationship like? - Very poor - Poor - Good - Very good	How important is the stakeholder to the club? -Not important - important -Vital	What can be done to improve the relationship over the next 12 months? (3 clear actions)

Resource Analysis

See Chapter 2 of the handbook for more details.

Resources	What you have at present	What you need in the future (3–5 years)

Vision Statement

See Chapter 2 of the handbook for more details.

Firstly, list the words you want to see in the vision statement:

1.

2.

3.

etc.

Now complete the sentences below:

In 20xx, our club will be ...

By 20xx, we want ...

By 20xx, we will have ...

Mission Statement

See Chapter 2 of the handbook for more details.

What do we do today?

How do we do it?

For whom do we do it?

What is the benefit?

Draft club mission:

Values Development

See Chapter 2 of the handbook for more details.

CORE VALUE	VALUE DEFINITION

SMART Objectives

See Chapter 2 of the handbook for more details.

Objective	Key Actions (list the key tasks under each objective)	Completion Date	Responsibility (who is the owner)	KPI/Measure (Target / Measurement)	WRAG (is it on schedule)

Progress/Outcome Key - RAG
- ☐ Not started, no action required
- 🟩 In progress and on track
- 🟧 In progress, some action required
- 🟥 Significant action required
- ⬛ Completed

Game-Day Experience

See Chapter 3 of the handbook for more details.

What did the research tell us about the game-day experience?

Areas we do well (and must continue to do well)
1.
2.
3.

Areas to improve
1.
2.
3.

Outline five actions that will help to improve the game-day experience:
1.
2.
3.
4.
5.

Code of Conduct (Coaches)

See Chapter 3 of the handbook for more details.

Coaches are required to:

- Respect the rights, dignity and worth of every person regardless of their gender, ability, cultural background or religion.
- Support, encourage and involve all players regardless of their talent level.
- Never ridicule or yell at players for errors or poor performance.
- Always consider the wellbeing and safety of participants before performance and results.
- Encourage participants to value their performances and not just results.
- Encourage and guide participants to accept responsibility for their own performance and behaviour both on and off the field.
- Maintain respectful and appropriate relationships with all participants.
- Ensure all activities are appropriate to the age, ability and experience of participants.
- Promote the positive aspects of the sport (e.g. fair play).
- Always respect the official's decision and support them to carry out their role.
- Display consistently high standards of good sporting behaviour and appearance.
- Follow all guidelines laid down by the national governing body and the club.
- Hold appropriate valid qualifications before commencing to coach.
- Never condone rule violations, unfair or unduly rough play or the use of prohibited substances.
- Never smoke or drink alcohol while in an official capacity.
- Never use offensive language or behaviour.
- Act as a role model at all times.

Code of Conduct (Players)

See Chapter 3 of the handbook for more details.

Players are required to:

- Respect the rights, dignity and worth of every person regardless of their gender, ability, cultural background or religion.
- Play by the rules and respect the official's decisions.
- Display good sporting behaviour at all times.
- Never use offensive language or behaviour towards anyone or engage in bullying of any person.
- Co-operate with your coach.
- Adhere to club policies including smoke-free areas and liquor license requirements.
- Never behave in a manner that would damage the reputation of the club either on or off the field.

Code of Conduct (Volunteers and Spectators)

See Chapter 3 of the handbook for more details.

Volunteers and **spectators** are required to:

- Act as good role models and ambassadors for the club at all times.
- Always welcome opposition players, spectators, officials etc. to the club.
- Never use offensive language or behaviour.
- Treat everyone including the opposition with respect regardless of their gender, ability, cultural background or religion.
- Display consistently high standards of good sporting behaviour including respecting the official's decisions.
- Adhere to the smoke-free policies of the club.
- Not to consume alcohol in any place other than where the club's license allows.
- Adhere to and support the club policies.

Training Session Planner

See Chapter 4 of the handbook for more details.

Focus of this session (what am i hoping to achieve?)

What equipment do I need?	
How many cones/markers?	
How many balls/bats/equipment?	
How many [coloured] BIBS?	

Warm up (describe the warm-up session)

Session 1 (describe and draw Session 1)

Session 2 (describe and draw Session 2)

Session 3 (describe and draw Session 3)

COOL DOWN (DESCRIBE AND DRAW THE COOL DOWN SESSION)

Coaches Qualification Record

See Chapter 4 of the handbook for more details.

Coaches Name	Current qualifications	Date of expiry	Current team coaching in the club	Training to be arranged and the training provider	Date for training

☑ Checklist for Starting a Women's Team

See Chapter 5 of the handbook for more details.

If you are thinking of starting a women's team at your club, you must consider the following:

		Answers
Competitions	Will the team(s) be entered into regional competition and at what age group?	
Recruitment	How will you attract new players and do you have a critical mass of players sufficient for training and fielding a squad already?	
Funding	Are there sources of local or regional funding available to you (i.e. grants, sponsorship, player fees)?	
Registration	Have you registered all players with the governing body?	
Fees	What membership fees will you charge, if any (perhaps you want to incentivise initially with zero fees)?	
Insurance	Is the team covered under the club's existing insurance policy?	
Game day	Are the facilities adequate for the women's team? Where will you play your home fixtures?	
Training	Has appropriate space been scheduled on the pitches/court for training sessions?	
Policies, procedures & forms	Have all the club policies, procedures and forms been updated to reflect the new women's squad?	

Community Engagement Checklist

See Chapter 7 of the handbook for more details.

1. **What objectives are you wanting to achieve?** ◆ What are the objectives? Are they achievable? Are the outcomes clearly defined with clear targets and milestones? How will you measure success?
Answers Objectives: ❖ ❖ ❖ How will we measure success? ❖ ❖ ❖
2. **Why are you doing this?** ◆ What is the purpose of the activity?
Answers ❖ ❖ ❖ ❖
3. **Who will be involved?** ◆ Who needs to be involved and why? Schools, community groups, charities etc. Explain what is expected.
Answers Who needs to be involved? ❖ ❖ What is expected? ❖ ❖

4.	**What level of relationship will be needed?**
	◆ Is it a light-touch relationship? (Don't pre-suppose the level of engagement that potential partners might want.)

Answers
What is the level of relationship?
- ❖
- ❖

5.	**What is the required timescale to deliver the agreed outcomes?**
	◆ What are the time constraints? Is the timetable realistic for all partners?

Answers
What are the time constraints?
- ❖
- ❖

6.	**What are the available resources?**
	◆ What are the resources required from the club to achieve the outcomes?

Answers
What are the resources required from the club?
- ❖
- ❖

7.	**How will you know that the objectives have been achieved?**
	◆ Has something improved?

Answers
How do we know if the objectives have been achieved?
- ❖
- ❖

Appendix **237**

Community Engagement Plan

See Chapter 7 of the handbook for more details.

Objective	Owner	Timeline	KPI	Key Actions	WRAG*

*WRAG - White (not yet started), Red (unlikely to be met), Amber (slightly behind completion), Green (on track for completion)

Note: this community engagement template should form part of your wider club development.

Brand Words

See Chapter 8 of the handbook for more details.

Brand words	Explanation (what does this brand word mean to us as a club)

Brand Checklist

See Chapter 8 of the handbook for more details.

Question	Answers
Have you created a brand guidelines document? ❖ Consistent colours to be used ❖ Consistent fonts to be used ❖ How the club logo should be applied	
What are the brand words? What does the club stand for?	
Do you have a clear brand tone of voice i.e. witty, playful, serious?	
Do you have a list of brand templates in place to ensure a consistent roll-out of your brand? ❖ Powerpoint visuals ❖ Club letterheaded document ❖ Email newsletter	
Does the content you post across digital platforms communicate your brand?	
What actions need to be taken to improve your club brand (identify three clear actions with an owner and deadline)?	

Annual Content Planner

See Chapter 8 of the handbook for more details.

	Lead Person Responsible	Web	WhatsApp	Email	Club App	Facebook	Instagram	X	YouTube	Other
Jan										
Feb										
Mar										
Apr										
May										
June										
July										
Aug										
Sept										
Oct										
Nov										
Dec										

Digital Inventory Checklist

See Chapter 8 of the handbook for more details.

Digital questions	Answer
Do you own your club branded URL?	
List out all the social platforms you are currently on?	
Which platforms have the most engagement (likes, shares, comments etc.)	
Have you the functionality to take online ads on the following platforms? ❖ Club website ❖ Club YouTube site ❖ Club app ❖ Other	
Does the club have a: ❖ Podcast ❖ Vlog ❖ Blog ❖ Other	
Does the club have an email database for the addresses of spectators, coaches, parents, players?	

Website Assessment Checklist

See Chapter 8 of the handbook for more details.

Area	Response
How long does it take for your website to download? ❖ Desktop ❖ Mobile Hint: Check out Google speed test.	
Is your website mobile phone friendly? Hint: Check out Google mobile friendly test site.	
Are there any broken links on your website? Hint: Check out Screaming Frog site to test links.	
Are you using keywords in your content on your website? Hint: Check out SEMRush for researching your keywords.	
Are links from partner sites to your website in place? Hint: Check out Moz.com to identify website linked to your website.	
Is the 'contact us' form up to date? Who receives this form?	
Have you all the tags in place – title tags, meta tags, alt tags? Hint: Check out SEMRush site for information on title tags, meta tags and alt tags.	
Are you posting content on your website on a regular basis (daily/weekly?)	
Is the structure of the website simple?	

Appendix 243

Event Calendar

See Chapter 8 of the handbook for more details.

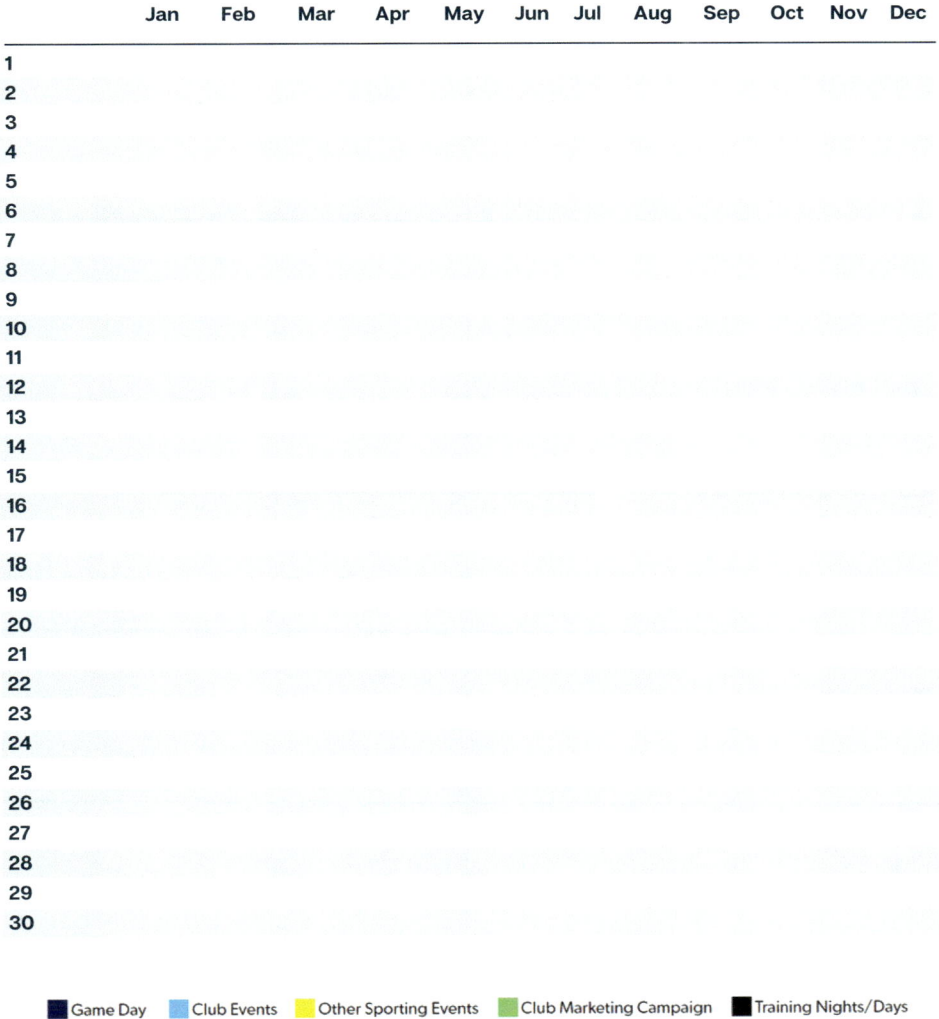

	Jan	Feb	Mar	Apr	May	Jun	Jul	Aug	Sep	Oct	Nov	Dec
1												
2												
3												
4												
5												
6												
7												
8												
9												
10												
11												
12												
13												
14												
15												
16												
17												
18												
19												
20												
21												
22												
23												
24												
25												
26												
27												
28												
29												
30												

■ Game Day   ■ Club Events   ■ Other Sporting Events   ■ Club Marketing Campaign   ■ Training Nights/Days

Post-event Evaluation

See Chapter 8 of the handbook for more details.

Question	Response
Did you meet your event objectives? If not, why not	
How many attended the event?	
What worked well?	
What did not work well?	
What feedback was obtained from attendees?	
Did the event break even or make a profit?	
What learnings can you take to future events?	

Game-Day Planner

See Chapter 8 of the handbook for more details.

GAME OPPONENT	
DATE / START TIME	

LOCAL TIME	ACTIVITY TO BE COMPLETED	PERSON RESPONSIBLE	✓

Income Generation Calendar

See Chapter 9 of the handbook for more details.

Income Stream	Fundraising	Sponsorship	Ticketing	Food & Beverage	Grants	Merchandise	Event income	Donations	Other
Person Responsible									
Jan									
Feb									
Mar									
Apr									
May									
June									
June									
Aug									
Sept									
Oct									
Nov									
Dec									
Total									

Sponsors Target List

See Chapter 9 of the handbook for more details.

Contact Name	Business Name	Position	Phone Number	Email Address	Date Contacted	Key contact in the club	Interested (Y/N)

Grant Identification

See Chapter 9 of the handbook for more details.

List the various community, foundations, local and national government grants	Do you meet the criteria? Y/N	How much funding can be secured? £/€/$	What can the funding be used for in the club - capital / infrastructure, programmes, equipment, etc.?

Facility Plan

See Chapter 10 of the handbook for more details.

Facility area	Work Required	Actions required	Owner	Deadline	Budget

Facility Usage Schedule

See Chapter 10 of the handbook for more details.

Team Name	Age Group	Day	Time (start & end time)	Venue Location (Training)	Lead Coach

Index

Note: Page references in *italics* refer to figures.

academy/youth committee 27; *see also* committee
academy/youth director 34–35
accident report form 214
accountability 3, 9, 36, 49, 66
account management 184; *see also* management
action log list 20, *21*, 211
action plans 70, 76–77; *see also* plan/planning
adult membership 175
adult men's/women's teams 98–99
adult player registration 175; *see also* players
agenda 14, 18, 20, 22, 24, 42, 75
AGM 13–15; agenda 14; announcement of 13–14; electing of board 14–15; membership fees 14; preparing reports 14; *see also* Special General Meetings (SGMs)
alcohol consumption 120–121
amateur sports 3, 28, 102
analysis: resource 58, *59*, 223; situation 61; stakeholder 58, *59*, 222; SWOT 58, *58*, 221
annual budget 25, 45, 46, 71, 72; *see also* budget/budgeting
annual content plan 153, *154*, 240 ; *see also* plan/planning
annual report 13–15, 46, 187; *see also* reporting
anti-drugs 121–123

appeal process 42
assets 29, 47–48, 180
assign fees 181
audit/auditing 45, 46, 201, 207; community 137; facilities 201–203; reporting and 45

balance sheet 46–47
bank account 11, 25, 46, 47
barbeque (BBQ) 31, 152, 177–178
bar/canteen revenue/food and beverages 177–178
behaviour 39, 87–89, 110, 124, 213, 229; coach 115; and professionalism 38; steps to improve *88*; types of 121
best practices 3, 20, 46, 48, 74, 101, 158, 200; *see also* professionalism
board 16–26; chairperson 22–23; club directors 26; club secretary 23–24; composition 16; diversity 17; electing of 14–15; key areas 17–18; members 17, 19; minutes 20–21; planning for 20; responsibilities 22–24; role of 16, 22–24; size 17; treasurer 25
brainstorming 188
brand/branding 143–171, 185; building 148; checklist *149*, 239; club 145–146, *146*; components of 145; content plan 152–155; database 160; developments 144–145, 148; email marketing 155–156; event management 165–170, *167*, *168*; marketing platforms 150; media

Index

communication 162–164; overview 143; positive image 148; process for 146, *146*; promoting club 150–160; promotional plan 151–152; social media 156–157; spectator and member engagement 160–161, *161*; strapline 144, 145, 148; values 148; website 158–159; words 238; *see also* communication

brilliant stewards 86–87

budget/budgeting *71*, 71–72; annual 25, 45, 46, 71, 72; event 166, *167*; template 166

bullying/anti-bullying 26, 38, 119, 121, 124, 125, 230

business: and community foundations 188; membership 175; to target 182–183

cash managing 47, 71

chairperson 17–18, 22–23; duties of 22; role of 22; traits of 22; *see also* board

changing rooms 66, 112, 201, 205

charitable incorporated organisation (CIO) 12

checklist 54; brand *149*, 239; club planning 54; community engagement 131–133, 139, 235–236; crisis management 164; digital inventory 241; governance 51; of policies 37–38, 212; pre-development plan 54, 218; safeguarding 39–40, 213; starting a women's team 113; training session 103; website assessment 159, 242; welcoming new members/players 80–81

child-safe organisation 38–39

clean and tidy spaces 83

club 204; administration 23–24, 43, 203; annual report 15; board members 17–19, 41; brand/branding 145–146, *146*; brochure 83; community 173; correspondence and communication 24; culture indicators 81; development plan 3–4, 53–55, *56*, 209, 219–220; directors 26; facilities 189, 199–207; female-friendly 112; female participation in 109–116; importance 9; information 80, 152–160; management 47, 156; members/membership in 13–15, 33–34; name 145; promoting 150–160; safeguarding 38–40; strong team spirit 91–92

club planning 53–77; action plans 70, 76–77; budgeting *71*, 71–72; checklist 54; coaching 60; creating *55*, 55–77, *56*; development 53–55, *56*; end of 77; goals 67–68; launching 74–75; measuring success 75–77; members/spectators 59–60; mission statement 64–65; organisational chart 72–73; overview 53; parent 60; player registration/membership data 58, 60, 61; research 59–62; resource 58, *59*; reviewing 76–77; SMART objectives 69–70; sponsorship 60; sport programmes 61; stakeholder 58, *59*; SWOT analysis 58, *58*; values 65–67; vision statement 63–64; WRAG column 76; writing 74; *see also* plan/planning

club secretary 23–24; duties of 23; role of 23; tasks of 24; traits of 24

club structures 11–34; board 16–26; club membership 13–15; committees 26–28; workforce/volunteer management 28–35

club treasurer 25; role of 25; traits of 25

coach/coaching 60, 98, 101–106, 115–116, 229; committee 27; communication 99; development 104–106; elite pyramid 102, *102*; female 115–116; overview 101; positive 101, 103; qualification record 233; steps to effective 106; training and education 104, *104*; *see also* players; training

code of conduct 17, 38, 39, 213, 229, 230, 231
colour palette 148
committee 18, 26–28, 111; academy/youth 27; composition of 28; facility 27; female 109–110; income 27, 174; promotions/media 27; role of 26; sporting/technical/coaching 27; suggested 26–27
communication 143–171; coach and players 99; crisis management 164; evaluation of 145; media 162–163; officer 33; with parents 89–90; press release 162, *163*; regular 98; technologies 125; *see also* brand/branding
community 186, 204; audit/auditing 137; clubs 173; focus 128–129, 139; foundations 188; local 128, 130–131; reach in 185; *see also* community engagement
community engagement 127–140, 196, 235–237; audit 137; checklist 131–133; conducting audit 137; create a *138*; focused 128–129, 139; importance of 129–130; local charity 134; local community 130–131, 135; local government 133–134, 136; needs of 135–136; overview 127; sports clubs 133; template *138*; *see also* community; relationships
competitive leagues 3
conducting research 60–61, 77; *see also* research
conflict/dispute resolution 41–42
conflict of interest 9, 42, *43*, 216
constitution 35–43, 110; accidents 40; code of conduct 38; conflict and dispute resolution 41–42; conflicts of interest 42–43; defined 35; safe environment and safeguarding members 38–39; *see also* policies
content management system (CMS) 158

content plan 152–155, 156–157; annual *154*; developing a 153; ideas for 153; *see also* plan/planning
contract sign 184
cost 69, 155, 175, 177, 181, 187, 192, 196, 207
crisis management 164
culture 111; coaching 101–106; indicators of club 81; representation 111; welcoming 82
cup winnings 196
customer service 31, 169, 177, 178

database 130, 152, 156, 158, 160, 193
data-collection 201
desk/desktop research 61, 136; *see also* research
digital inventory checklist 241
document 13, 14, 20, 28, 37–39, 45, 49, 74, 83, 136, 148, 184, 187, 203–205
donations/patronage 47, 175, 177, 190

elite pyramid 102, *102*
email content 155
email header 155
email marketing 155–156
emergency details form 215
emergency plan 166; *see also* plan/planning
engaging young people 18
ethics 17
event calendar 143, 168, *168*, 184, 243
event management 165–170, *167*; budgeting 166, *167*; calendar 168, *168*; emergency situations 166; game-day planner 170, *170*; post-event evaluation *169*; template 166; ways to create 167–168; *see also* brand/branding
experience 79–99; brilliant stewards 86–87; clean and tidy spaces 83; club brochure 83; communication with parents 89–90; game day 84–85, 228; improving 83–94; inclusion and

diversity 93–94; positive coaching 103; right environment 87–88; strong team spirit 91–92; tournament 84–85; underage and adult teams links 91; voluntary stewards 86–87; *see also* welcoming club
expertise 18, 131, 185
external plan 74; *see also* plan/planning

facilities 192; audit 201–203; changing rooms 205; clubs 199–207; committee 27 (*see also* committee); insurance 206–207; lighting 205; local council 200–201; maintenance 205–207; management plan 203–205; overview 199; owning/leasing 200; plan *202*; strategic plan 204–205; toilet 205; usage 203, *203*
family membership 175
female committee 109–110; *see also* committee
female participation: attracting more 114; in club 109–116; coaching 115–116; friendly sporting facilities 111–112; gender-balanced leadership 110; healthy and active 109; overview 109; representation 109–111; sport week 114
final review meeting 184–185
finance 44–49; annual budget 46; audited accounts 46; balance sheet 47; bank account 46; cash managing 47; committee 45; disclosure 45; growth 196; information 58; insurance 48; management 44–45; mismanagement 9; monthly/quarterly reports 46; personal 47; procurement 48–49; reporting and auditing 45; routine set up 47; tax 47–48
fixture secretary/registrar 33
focus community 128–129, 139; *see also* community
focus groups 59–61, 135
food and beverages 177–178, 192

formal complaint 41
friendly sporting facilities 111–112
fundraising 15, 25, 134, 153, 165, 168, 174, 178–179, 180, 202

gambling addiction 123–124
game-day experience 85, 144, 228
game-day planner 84–85, 170, *170*, 245; *see also* plan/planning
game fees 196
gender-balanced leadership 110
general administration 24
General Data Protection Regulations (GDPR) 43
goals 46, 53, 67–68, 71–75, 156, 167, 196, 200; *see also* vision
governance 110; and admin 9–51; board 16–26; checklist 51; club membership 13–15; concept of 10; constitution and policies 35–43; controls 44–50; defined 9; finance 44–49; legal compliance 43–44; legal status 11–12; overview 9; pillars/foundations 10; risk management 49–50; standards 47; structures 13–34; workforce/volunteer management 28–35
governing body 13, 22–24, 36, 42, 43, 48, 58, 103–105, 199, 229
grant identification 248
grants and foundations 185–189, *188*; applications unsuccessful 186; applying for 188–189; business and community foundations 188; city and local government/region 186; national government/province 187
grassroots pyramid 102, *102*

health/active living 109
health grants 186
holiday camps 58, 116, 133, 175, 192

incident dealing 123, *123*
inclusion and diversity 93–94

income 173–196; bar/canteen revenue/food and beverages 177–178; city/regional government 186; club facilities 189; donations/patronage 190; fundraising 178–179; generation calendar 246; generation committee 27, 174; generation process 179, *179*; grants and foundations 185–189; holiday camps 192; membership 175, *176*; merchandise 195; money generation 173; online digital revenue 190; other sources 196; overview 173; planning 174; sponsorship 180–185; streams 174–196; ticketing 193–194
informal discussion 41
information gathering 61
insurance 24, 48, 71, 166, 192, 206–207; *see also* liability insurance
inventory and equipment 204

job description 28–29, 73
junior player registration 175

key performance indicators (KPIs) 187
kick-off meeting 184; *see also* meetings

launching plan 74–75; *see also* plan/planning
leadership 22, 38, 109, 110, 130
legal compliance 43–44, 51
legal status 3, 11–12, 51
liability insurance 192, 207; *see also* insurance
lighting 112, 119, 205
limited company 11–12
local charity 134
local community 49, 64, 94, 95, 116, 125, 127–135, 143, 144; *see also* community
local council 131, 200–201
local government 11, 48, 133–134, 136, 186, 200
logo 144, 145, 148, 155, 167, 180, 195
long-term survival 3; *see also* strategic planning

management 44–45; account 184; approval 204; club/cash 47, 156; crisis 164; event 165–170; finance 44–45; plan 203–205; risk 49–50; workforce/volunteer 28–35
marketing platforms 148, 150, 192
measuring success 75–77
media committee 27; *see also* committee
media communication 162–163; *see also* communication
media valuation 181
meetings 11, 22, 24, 33, 91, 104, 128
member engagement 160–161, *161*
membership 14, 175, *176*; *see also* registration fee
mentoring 34, 110
merchandise 152, 153, 155, 189, 192, 195
minutes secretary 20–21, 24
mission development 65
mission statement 64–65, 225
mobile optimised 156
money generation 173; *see also* income
monthly/quarterly reports 46
multi-use games area (MUGA) 205

national government/province 187
non-competitive leagues 3

old age pensioners (OAPs) 194
online/digital revenue 190, *191*
organisational chart 72–73
organisation facilities 204; *see also* facilities
owning/leasing 200

pantone 145
parents 60; communication with 89–90; engaging 90; and members 98
performance appraisals 18, 22
personal finance 47; *see also* finance
personalised thanks 31

plan/planning 174; action 70; annual content 153, *154*, 240; for board 20; community engagement 237; content 152–155; emergency 166; external 74; game-day 84–85, 170, *170*, 245; income 174; launching 74–75; promotional 151–152; reviewing 76–77; strategic 24, 57–58, 71, 136; succession 18; *see also* club planning

players 60, 230; communication 99; recruitment 95–96; registration/membership data 58, 61, 175; retention 97–99; youth 89–90, 96, 153, 192; *see also* coach/coaching

policies 35–43, 111; checklist of 37–38, 212; and procedures 37–38; safeguarding 39; social media 157; team 207; welfare 120–125; *see also* constitution

positive experience 98; *see also* experience

positive image 148, 158, 185

post-event evaluation *169*, 244

pre-development plan 54, 218

pre-season training 99

press release 75, 144, 162, *163*

procurement 45, 48–49

professionalism 3, 38, 49, 66, 83, 121; *see also* best practices

promotion 27, 95, 132, 150–160, 192, 193

protecting club 119–125; alcohol consumption 120–121; anti-bullying 121; anti-drugs 121–123; anti-gambling 123–124; anti-racism 124–125; drugs abuse 122; overview 119; safeguarding 125; smoking 120; welfare policies 120–125

Public and Communications Officer (PCO) 145

public relations (PR) 181, 182

public relations officer (PRO) 33, 166

questionnaires 60

racism 119, 124–125

recreational drug use 122

recruit/recruitment 18–19, 29, 34, 39, 96, 99, 110, 213; advertise and promote 95; brilliant stewards 86–87; coach 96; comfortable welcome 96; current 95; fun/easy to engage 96; local opportunities 95; players/members 80–81, 95–96; volunteers 32

registration fee 174, 175, 192

relationships 185; with council 200–201; local charity 134; local community 130–131, 135; local council 200–201; local government 133–134; sports clubs 133; symbiotic 102; *see also* community engagement

reporting 14, 39, 45, 213; *see also* annual report

representation 109–111; constitution 110; culture 111; female committee 109–110; increasing female 110–111; pathways 111; policies 111; practicalities 110; recruitment/training/retention 110; role models and mentoring 110; transparency 111; *see also* female participation

research 59–62; conducting 60–61, 77; desk 61, 136; and focus groups 59–61; gathering information 61; surveys 61–62

resource 3, 5, 9, 21, 29, 58, *59*, 157, 223; *see also* volunteers

retain players 97–99; adult men's and women's teams 98–99; tips to improve 98–99; *see also* players

reviewing plan 76–77; *see also* plan/planning

right environment 87–88

risk management 49–50

risk register 50, 217

robust governance framework 36

routine set up 47

safe environment 38–39
safeguarding 38–40, 125, 213; members 38–39; officer 39, 213; policy 39, 213
sales outlets 194
sales presentation 181–182
screening volunteers 32; *see also* volunteers
search engine optimisation (SEO) 158
semi-professional sports clubs 3, 86, 121, 173, 190
situation analysis 61; *see also* analysis
skills: based boards 16; organisation 109; teaching 101; team 103; of volunteer coordinator 31
SMART objectives 62, 69, *69*, 69–70, 227
smoking 86, 119, 120, 125
social media 95, 116, 144, 156–157, 193, 195; channels 156; components of 157; policy 157
social occasion 199
spam words 155
Special General Meetings (SGMs) 13; *see also* AGM
spectators 37, 38, 59–60, 80, 84, 86–88, 134, 144, 152, 155–156, 160–161, *161*, 177, 231
sponsorship 60, 130, 167, 180–185, 190, 192
sponsors target list 183, 247
sporting/technical/coaching committee 27; *see also* committee
sport programmes 61
sports packages 181
sport week 114
stakeholders 46, 58, *59*, 74, 144, 205, 222
strapline 144–145, 148; *see also* brand/branding
strategic planning 24, 57, 71, 136, 204–205; *see also* long-term survival
strong team spirit 91–92
subject line 155
succession planning 18; *see also* plan/planning
surveys 58, 61–62, 84, 135, 137, 168, 185
sustainability 196
SWOT analysis 58, *58*, 221; *see also* analysis

tax 47–48; *see also* finance
team spirit 91–92, 98, 106
template: event budget 166; event calendar 168, *168*; game day planner 170, *170*; post-event evaluation 169, *169*; strategic objectives 69
terms of reference (ToR) 28
text 80, 96, 145, 156
ticketing 175, 193–194
toilet facility 205
tone of voice 145
tournament 3, 48, 58, 79, 84–86, 92, 165, 180, 196, 207
training 39, 213; bonus 31; for club volunteers 30; and education 104, *104*; session planner 232; *see also* coach/coaching
transparency 3, 9, 10, 15, 36, 37, 111
typography 145, 148

underage/adult teams 91
unincorporated association 12
unsubscribe link 155

values 65–67, 145; brand 148; development 66–67, 226
vision: development 63–64; statement 63–64, 224
voluntary stewards 86–87
volunteers 3, 5, 15, 18, 22, 23, 29, 38, 53, 65, 79, 88, 95, 98, 120, 129, 231; awards 31; collectively 30; coordinator 29–31; for external awards 31; in person 30; recruiting new 32; screening 32; thanking 30–31; training 30; *see also* resource

website 95, 158–159, 242
weekly training programme 99
welcoming club 79–99; create a *82*; indicators 81; overview 79; recruit new players/members 80–81, 95–96; retain players 97–99; *see also* experience
welfare officer 33
welfare policies 120–125; *see also* policies
women's team 98–99, *113*, 234; *see also* female participation

workforce/volunteer management 28–35; academy/youth director 34–35; coordinator 29; fixture secretary/registrar 33; job description 28–29; PRO 33; thanking 30–31; training for 30; welfare officer 33; workload 29
workload sharing 4, 29; *see also* volunteers
WRAG column 76
writing development plan 14, 42, 74

youth players 89–90, 96, 153, 192; *see also* players

For Product Safety Concerns and Information please contact our
EU representative GPSR@taylorandfrancis.com Taylor & Francis
Verlag GmbH, Kaufingerstraße 24, 80331 München, Germany